Disrupting Sports Journalism

This book critically explores the impact that digital technology has had on the practices and norms of sports journalism.

In the wake of major digital disruptions in news reporting, the author analyses how sports journalism has been particularly vulnerable to challenges and attacks on its expertise because of its historically weak commitment to professionalism. Ultimately, an argument is built that sports journalism's professional distinctiveness will depend on its capacity to produce rigorous news work at a time when its core, routinised practices are being displaced by bloggers and team media. Recent developments such as The Athletic, a start-up that has built its business model around quality sports storytelling, and the impact of the COVID-19 pandemic offer hope that a paradigm shift in digital sports journalism culture towards serious reporting is starting to emerge. The question for both the industry and scholars going forward is whether these changes will crystallise and take hold in the long term.

Disrupting Sports Journalism is a valuable text for researchers and students in sports media and journalism studies, as well as for industry professionals seeking an insight into developments in the field.

Simon McEnnis is principal lecturer in the School of Art and Media at the University of Brighton. He researches sports journalism professionalism in the digital age and his articles have appeared in journals including *Digital Journalism, Journalism* and *Journalism Practice*. He has a professional journalism background, having worked with local and national newspapers.

Disruptions: Studies in Digital Journalism
Series editor: Bob Franklin

Disruptions refers to the radical changes provoked by the affordances of digital technologies that occur at a pace and on a scale that disrupts settled understandings and traditional ways of creating value, interacting and communicating both socially and professionally. The consequences for digital journalism involve far reaching changes to business models, professional practices, roles, ethics, products and even challenges to the accepted definitions and understandings of journalism. For Digital Journalism Studies, the field of academic inquiry which explores and examines digital journalism, disruption results in paradigmatic and tectonic shifts in scholarly concerns. It prompts reconsideration of research methods, theoretical analyses and responses (oppositional and consensual) to such changes, which have been described as being akin to 'a moment of mind-blowing uncertainty'.

Routledge's new book series, **Disruptions: Studies in Digital Journalism**, seeks to capture, examine and analyse these moments of exciting and explosive professional and scholarly innovation which characterize developments in the day-to-day practice of journalism in an age of digital media, and which are articulated in the newly emerging academic discipline of Digital Journalism Studies.

Reappraising Local and Community News in the UK
Media, Practice and Policy
David Harte and Rachel Matthews

Disrupting Sports Journalism
Simon McEnnis

Disruption and Digital Journalism
Assessing News Media Innovation in a Time of Dramatic Change
John V. Pavlik

For more information, please visit: www.routledge.com/Disruptions/book-series/DISRUPTDIGJOUR

Disrupting Sports Journalism

Simon McEnnis

LONDON AND NEW YORK

First published 2022
by Routledge
2 Park Square, Milton Park, Abingdon, Oxon OX14 4RN

and by Routledge
605 Third Avenue, New York, NY 10158

Routledge is an imprint of the Taylor & Francis Group, an informa business

© 2022 Simon McEnnis

The right of Simon McEnnis to be identified as author of this work has been asserted in accordance with sections 77 and 78 of the Copyright, Designs and Patents Act 1988.

All rights reserved. No part of this book may be reprinted or reproduced or utilised in any form or by any electronic, mechanical, or other means, now known or hereafter invented, including photocopying and recording, or in any information storage or retrieval system, without permission in writing from the publishers.

Trademark notice: Product or corporate names may be trademarks or registered trademarks, and are used only for identification and explanation without intent to infringe.

British Library Cataloguing-in-Publication Data
A catalogue record for this book is available from the British Library

Library of Congress Cataloging-in-Publication Data
A catalog record has been requested for this book

ISBN: 978-0-367-61862-9 (hbk)
ISBN: 978-0-367-61867-4 (pbk)
ISBN: 978-1-003-10686-9 (ebk)

DOI: 10.4324/9781003106869

Typeset in Times New Roman
by Taylor & Francis Books

Dedicated to Rosina, Louisa and Peter, with special mention to Wilbur the dog for the 5am wake-up calls

Contents

Acknowledgements   ix

1   Introduction: Sports journalists and the professional crisis   1

    Aims of the book 4
    Theoretical orientation of the book 6
    Outline of the book 9

2   Digital sports journalism   12

    Digital disruption to traditional practice 13
    The emergence of the digital sports journalist 18
    Digital sports journalism: Innovation or churnalism? 20
    Conclusion 23

3   Sports blogging   27

    Blogging as alternative sports journalism 28
    Sports journalism and acceptable blogging 33
    Stay out of the press box: Protecting boundaries from bloggers 35
    Blurring of boundaries: The sports journalist as blogger 38
    Conclusion 40

4   Sports public relations   42

    Inside out: The changing boundaries of access 44
    From sources to rivals: The rise of team media 47

Pushing back: Sports journalism's acts of resistance 51
Conclusion 54

5   Athlete sports journalism 57

Print versus broadcast sports journalism 58
The rise of athlete sports journalism 61
Conclusion 66

6   The Athletic 69

The Athletic's disruptive business model 69
The Athletic's journalists get to (rhetorical) work 72
Thinking outside the press box: The Athletic and
  professional practice 76
Conclusion 79

7   COVID-19 and sports journalism 82

Back on the beat: Journalism and the return of sport 85
Exclusive access: Sports journalists in empty stadiums 87
The Athletic 89
Conclusion 91

8   Conclusion: Future considerations 94

The future of access: All, some or no areas? 96
Sports journalism: An evolving professional field? 97
Final thoughts 99

References 101
Index 118

Acknowledgements

Sincere thanks to Professor Bob Franklin, the series editor, for initiating, guiding and reviewing this project. It has been a pleasure and a privilege to contribute this book to the *Disruptions: Studies in Digital Journalism* series. Thanks also to my excellent colleagues in the University of Brighton journalism department, Ben Parsons and Owen Evans, for their fantastic support in the day job that has allowed me to write this book alongside it.

1 Introduction
Sports journalists and the professional crisis

Sports journalism is a curious occupation in that the perceived glamour and desirability in being paid to watch events for free from press boxes is undermined by a poor professional reputation, which has led to it being dubbed as the 'toy' department of the news media. Sports journalism is regarded as "a department focused on frivolity and continuous promotion rather than being a serious part of the fourth estate" (Daum & Scherer, 2018, p. 553). Certainly, sports journalists were already wrestling with professional insecurity and striving to raise their standing when the digital age dawned. Salwen and Garrison (1998), writing as the internet and mobile technology started to become more widely accessible, found in surveys and interviews with US sports journalists that professionalism, ahead of job security, was the principal concern. The US sportscaster Howard Cosell, who invoked the term the 'toy department' in critiquing his own profession, later retracted this claim. Cosell was representing an emerging view within sports journalism that its subject matter had become more serious and roles were increasingly requiring a mastery of more complex knowledge and analytical skills. Cosell stated:

> The essential point is that sports are no longer fun and games, that they are everywhere – in people's minds, in conversation, in the importance we attach to it – and that they can affect the basics of our lives (to wit, the part of our taxes that may be directed to supporting a sports franchise, without our ever knowing it). Once I bought the Jimmy Cannon dictum that "Sports is the Toy Department of life." I don't now and never will again.
> (Cosell, 1985, p. 16)

However, sports journalists' attempts to elevate their status and standing have been rendered more challenging and complex in the digital age. Lowes and Robillard (2018) note that "no change has had a more

DOI: 10.4324/9781003106869-1

significant impact on the relationship between sports journalists and the teams they cover than the rise of digitization" (p. 316), while Buzzelli, Gentile, Billings and Sadri (2020) argue the most significant impact of the globalisation of sports is "the role of digital technology on the experience of producing and consuming mediated sports content" (p. 1516). Sports journalists are experiencing fundamental, existential concerns in that their professional base is threatened by new actors who have adopted its norms, practices, codes, routines and values. The very essence of sports journalists' expertise is now under scrutiny. In this sense, sports journalists have much in common with their wider newsroom colleagues. As Anderson (2008) states:

> American journalism ... enters the twenty-first century beset on all sides. Journalists' tenuous role as experts in determining "all the news that's fit to print" is under fire. At the same time, bloggers, online journalists, and other ordinary citizens and writers are attacking the very idea that there is any sort of journalistic expertise at all.
>
> (Anderson, 2008, p. 248)

Sports journalism is particularly vulnerable to an attack on its expertise in the digital age. Shifts brought about by digital technology have prompted serious questions about the nature of sports journalists' value and distinctiveness, and whether their authority and privilege in society are warranted. Sports journalists perceive their experience in attending sports events and being a first-hand eyewitness to the spectacle as pivotal to expertise (McEnnis, 2013). However, the fans who regularly attend sports events can also communicate their thoughts and observations, while armchair viewers now have access to a proliferation of live, televised sport that allows them to produce their own opinion and analysis, even though they are not physically present. As part of their toy department reputation, sports journalists have been dismissed as 'fans with typewriters' or 'fans with notebooks', favouring subjectivity, partisanship and opinion over objectivity, impartiality and hard news. Fans now actually do have typewriters and notebooks, metaphorically speaking, in their access to digital and social media platforms. Supporters can create their own narratives through formats such as message boards, tweets and blogs (Kian, Burden & Shaw, 2011; McCarthy, 2012, 2014). Sports journalists consider a bulging contacts book to be evidence of professional acumen, yet fans can also know club insiders who give them access to players and coaches for their blogs and websites (McEnnis, 2016).

Introduction 3

Sports journalism is organised around a beat system that involves regularly attending press conferences and briefings that supply a ready and reliable stream of information (Sherwood, Nicholson & Marjoribanks, 2017a). The beat system is structured according to geographical areas or specific sports, and often involves a narrow source environment in which sports journalists are highly reliant on the same few gatekeepers to perform news work. This model creates a dependency on media managers who control the access and accreditation of sports journalists. What used to be a rather balanced relationship, in which clubs and organisations relied on sports journalists for the oxygen of publicity, has given way to a lop-sided power dynamic whereby these gatekeepers now have their own digital and social media channels and are therefore less reliant on independent media. The fact that sports journalists operate in highly controlled environments and have narrow source relations means they face enormous pressure to produce promotional, complicit and unquestioning stories for fear of having their access revoked. Sports journalists are therefore open to accusations of being merely "cheerleaders" for sports clubs and organisations. Here, sports journalists are accused of lacking professional distance from their sources and failing to exercise critical application to the stories and events they cover. Sports clubs and organisations' own digital channels, known as team media, are overtly providing a 'cheerleader' function by producing highly positive stories that are effectively a public-relations exercise. Sports journalists consider their insider access as important to expertise since it makes certain information available to a privileged few. This insider status, however, pales by comparison with sources themselves that are producing and generating their own stories and media.

Sports journalism is also seeing changes to its internal character and composition that are disrupting professional cohesiveness. Sports journalism's practices and personnel have expanded as news organisations attempt to cover multiple digital and social media platforms, often in addition to analogue channels such as newspapers and television. The different actors who have emerged within sports journalism's occupational group have expanded the boundaries of skills, approaches and practices. Sports journalists' traditional notions of expertise revolve around being embedded within professional sport, which is why social and interviewing skills are so highly valued within the occupational community. However, digitally native sport journalists are rejecting the notion that fieldwork is the only way to conduct news work. These office-based positions are sourcing stories not from direct human contacts but from a networked, internet environment. Further, digital journalists build parasocial relations with audiences, who provide

4 Introduction

content by contributing to discussion or posting thoughts below web stories, in the building of an online community that, in turn, cultivates brand loyalty. Digitally native sports journalists are also curating and combining content from other forms of media, such as pundits' comments on television and YouTube videos of past sporting exploits. These routines and practices do not require insider access and knowledge, source relations within professional sport, interviewing skills or acquiring first-hand information. They therefore challenge the very foundations of sports journalism at a time when the occupation is trying to assert the importance and cohesion of its professional work in the face of boundary challenges from outsiders. These concerns are also informed by the commercial challenges of the news industry, which has struggled to financially adapt to digital technology. The resulting consolidation of the news business has led to reduced staff needing to produce more content over digital platforms that are neither constrained by space nor time.

Aims of the book

Hutchins and Rowe (2012) describe sports journalism as a 'leaking craft' in which the "once relatively robust habitus ... has turned fragile and permeable" (p. 150). This book explores how the boundaries of sports journalism have expanded and the consequences of this growth for the professional group's survival. It attempts to establish the exact nature of this increasing porousness of sports journalism's boundaries and to identify the new actors who are contributing to sports journalism and/or challenging the professional field. It analyses how sports journalists are simultaneously trying to defend their distinctiveness in justifying and maintaining their privileged position as "key cultural narrators" (Boyle, Rowe & Whannel, 2009, p. 251) while pursuing a professional project that involves elevating standards and dispelling the 'toy department' reputation. The book considers whether sports journalists are still clinging to their traditional notions of expertise, even though they have essentially been displaced by factors external to the professional field and undermined by changes that are internal to it, or whether they are re-articulating the professional contribution.

So how exactly can sports journalism close down the toy department? The concept of proper and serious sports journalism will be used in this book to refer to expectations around the contribution to society. Serious sports journalism can, however, be challenging to define and can mean different things in different contexts (Weedon, Wilson, Yoon & Lawson, 2016). This book distils the concept of serious sports journalism as consisting of three essential elements, which rather than being separate and distinct may be overlapping and connected. First, it speaks to journalism's normative view of itself, which is to hold power to account. To achieve this, sports journalism must carve out a degree of independence and autonomy from its sources, namely the professional sport environment, and develop an inquisitiveness and a determination in finding and unearthing the truth. Second, sports journalism should place sport into a wider political, social, economic and historical context that involves providing depth and rigour to its reporting. Third, sports journalism ought to be socially responsible in the way that it offers a public service, which involves ensuring minority voices and marginal groups are heard, and that multiple perspectives are sourced while monitoring and advocating for social justice in sport. Proper and serious journalism is only achievable if its practitioners demonstrate a strong commitment to professional principles such as objectivity, autonomy, independence and public service (Deuze, 2005).

This book provides a critical exploration of these issues by examining and evaluating previous research findings, industry discourse, case studies and critical incidents. It focuses predominantly on UK and US journalism because major-league sport in these territories has become increasingly globalised. Meanwhile, journalism has become international in outlook as news organisations seek to exploit the digital opportunities to grow audiences and advertisers. However, this book will also refer to other national contexts where relevant, as sports journalism operates in a shared community of practice in which its professional aims, motivations, aspirations, concerns and challenges are widespread (Hutchins & Boyle, 2017).

This text reflects the fact that the effects of digital technologies have been at the forefront of sports journalism research, in the form of journal articles and book chapters that have looked at specific areas, such as blogging, team media and online news work. This book knits these disparate threads together to produce a comprehensive and critical overview of how digital technology has disrupted sports journalism. There are few academic books specifically on sports journalism. Raymond Boyle's *Sports Journalism: Context and Issues* (2006) remains an important go-to text in establishing a clear critical framework but pre-dates social media. Tom Bradshaw and Daragh Minogue's (2019) book, *Sports Journalism: The State of Play*, provides a wide-ranging, non-digitally specific overview of shifts in sports journalism practice that includes intersections with diversity, law, regulation and politics.

Theoretical orientation of the book

Professionalism is an important concept in journalism studies that makes sense of the changes that journalists have undergone in the digital age (Aldridge & Evetts, 2003; Anderson & Schudson, 2008; Carlson, 2017; Carlson & Lewis, 2015; Lewis, 2012; Waisbord, 2013). Journalism is recognisably professional in its claims to be providing a service to the public and its adherence to a code of conduct, such as ethics, regardless of the industry's own protestations that it has historically rejected it in favour of "such nomenclature as occupation, craft, or vocation" (Carlson, 2017, p. 32). Carlson (2017) adds that "professionalism best captures the declaration journalists make about the social value and specificity of their work" (p. 33). However, the journalism industry is recognising that a discourse of professionalism can be an important boundary marker in the digital age when confronted by other actors who have adopted its norms, styles and forms (Waisbord, 2013). Further, the growth in graduate level entry to journalism means that its workers will be increasingly interested in professional respectability (Aldridge & Evetts, 2003). Journalism is a particularly fascinating profession to study because of its anomalous position in rejecting the traditional characteristics of occupational closure, such as licensing and clear entry qualifications (Aldridge & Evetts, 2003). Journalists have instead preferred to pursue a discourse of press freedom that has inadvertently left its professional boundaries open to challenge and contestation in the digital age.

Journalism professionalism, then, is concerned with how journalists attempt to maintain, protect and even elevate their status as a distinct professional collective that possesses exclusive rights to a particular domain of work. In drawing on four broad concepts from the sociology of work and professions – Larson's professional project, Abbott's jurisdictional control, Bourdieu's field theory and Gieryn's boundary work – scholars attempt to track both the changing internal and external composition of the field. Larson's (1977) notion of the professional project provides a sense of purpose to the theory in the way that professionalism is used as leverage to obtain greater status, recognition and, crucially, resources. Abbott's (1988) concept of 'jurisdictions', in which occupational groups seek to control expert knowledge and therefore the right to perform particular tasks and work in society, suggests that professionalism is mainly motivated by the threat of competition. Of journalism, Abbott (1988) states: "The clearest force driving reporters towards a formal conception of their jurisdiction was in fact competition with hired publicity agents" (p. 225). Bourdieu's (1993, 2005) concept of fields is similar to jurisdiction although it also recognises the importance of internal competition in shaping a field. Here, journalism can be considered as a site of struggle in which different actors compete for power. Wall (2019) states that "the habitus of traditional journalism is seen in formulaic writing practices, such as quoting sources and attribution of information … relying on the power elite for information as a way to establish credibility" (p. 5). However, this notion of journalism's habitus is becoming increasingly challenged by newer digital roles and practices.

Both concepts of jurisdiction and field theory can be more closely demarcated by what Gieryn (1983) describes as boundary work. For Gieryn, boundary work is a discursive and rhetorical act that is about creating a public image through the self-promotion of skills, knowledge and expertise. Here, Gieryn is interested in both intra- and inter-professional struggle. He explores how, in the 19th century, science ousted religion as the principal belief system in society through discursive boundary work whereby leading scientists would, in public talks and publications, extol the virtues of science while denigrating religious belief. However, within science, there was a battle for what constituted good practice. For instance, anatomists pushed phrenology, which connected physiology to personality and religious belief, outside of science's boundaries through public descriptions that transformed it from "serious science to sideshow legerdemain" (Gieryn, 1983, p. 788). Anatomists denounced phrenologists because they thought their authority, access to resources, reputation and resources were being threatened. Phrenologists were also delegitimised through their exclusion from key positions in scientific organisations, lectures and debates.

Similarly, journalism is a discursive battleground in which different professional sub-cultures compete to define the occupation's values and norms. Zelizer (1992) notes how discursive boundary work around the Kennedy assassination was instrumental in how television journalists, as relatively new entrants into the field, were able to establish themselves as cultural authorities over their more established print counterparts. In sports journalism, the 'quality' broadsheet culture of in-depth analysis and context has vied with the popular, tabloid virtues of speed and breaking news for supremacy. That digital technology has led to both internal and external challenges to sports journalism's boundaries means a more intensified and diverse rhetorical battleground now plays out not just in Gieryn's public talks of the 19th century or Zelizer's (1992) "printed press, professional and trade reviews, television retrospectives, film documentaries and books" (p. 11) of the 20th century, but also in tweets and blog posts that happen in real time and in interactive ways.

In the absence of professional structures, Gieryn's concept of discursive boundary work becomes significant to the ways that journalists convince the public of their expertise and authority. Journalism is therefore not about the stories that are produced but how journalists talk about the stories they produce. As Aldridge and Evetts (2003, p. 560) note, "journalism is an intensely reflexive occupation which constantly talks to and about itself" and that professionalism is:

> a discourse of self-control, even self-belief, an occupational badge or marker which gives meaning to the work and enables workers to justify and emphasize the importance of their work to themselves and others.
>
> (Aldridge & Evetts, 2003, p. 555)

Carlson (2015) has developed a schematic for journalism boundary work that applies Gieryn's three dimensions of expansion, expulsion and protection of autonomy as they relate to participants, practices and professionalism. Here, journalism has expanded to accommodate citizen journalism as participants, social media practices and new media as an acceptable publishing platform. However, journalists who fabricate stories and practices considered damaging and unethical, such as paparazzi photography, are expelled.

This book is mindful of Carlson's (2015) framework in its exploration of sports journalism as a field that is being reconstructed and reconfigured by new actors. How sports journalists patrol their professional boundaries, who is threatening them and who gets to define the codes, values and practices is of immense importance to understanding a key specialism in journalism that is vital to the revenue of news organisations. As English (2016) notes, "sport sits predominantly on the economic capital side of the axis in the journalistic field" (p. 1004). Journalism professionalism studies tend to focus on the news desk and do not automatically map on to sports journalism, which has its own beliefs, values and routines even if it shares what Deuze (2005) describes as an occupational ideology of ethics, objectivity, autonomy and public service with a broader community of practice.

Sports journalism studies have grown as scholars have responded to the increasing economic significance of sports. The 'toy department' label has also become an important concept in research into sports journalism. It has emerged as a useful point of departure for scholars who have been seeking to both critique and re-assess sports journalism's professional standards in the digital age (Boyle, 2006; Cassidy, 2017; Oates & Pauly, 2007; Rowe, 2007; Salwen & Garrison, 1998). Sports journalism researchers have focused on various strands in the digital age, whether that be digital practice, source relations or blogging. This book pulls these disparate themes together to paint a comprehensive picture of the ways in which digital technology has led to significant disruption for sports journalism. In doing so, this book's stance is one of social constructionism rather than technological determinism in the way that it is focused on how digital technology is being used by different groups of actors to provide professional and boundary challenges to sports journalism.

Outline of the book

This book is structured according to two broad areas that reflect both the internal (Chapter 2: Digital sports journalism, Chapter 5: Athlete sports journalism, Chapter 6: The Athletic) and external challenges (Chapter 3: Sports blogging, Chapter 4: Sports public relations) to sports journalism's professionalism. Chapter 7 (COVID-19 and sports journalism) considers how COVID-19 has informed sports journalism's professional trajectory.

Specifically, Chapter 2 analyses how digital technology has expanded both the boundaries of practice and personnel in sports journalism. It considers how traditional sports journalists have incorporated digital and social media into their work routines and the implications of this paradigm shift on their ability to produce serious news work. It also discusses the emergence of the digitally native sports journalist, who is bringing new practices and interpretations of principle to the occupational group. However, these new ways of approaching sports journalism can contradict important values and beliefs within the occupational group, such as covering sport from TV feeds rather than being present at the stadium and using digital and social media as a source of information rather than developing human contacts with professional sport personnel. This departure challenges historical understandings of sports journalism and has led to an internal tension and division within news organisations between the digitally native and beat sports journalist and what constitute legitimate and acceptable practices.

Chapter 3 contemplates how blogging is challenging the notion of sports journalism as a professional domain. Actors have entered the journalistic field from other professional fields, such as law and finance, to provide a deeper understanding of sport issues. Sports journalists have attempted to control the blogosphere by integrating certain accepted forms of blogging into the mainstream that help to increase the story count of news websites relatively cheaply. However, the fluidity of journalists and bloggers moving in and out of professional and amateur spaces has blurred boundaries and complicated definitions of expertise. It has also led to multiple perspectives and raised interesting questions for who actually produces serious news work and under what conditions and motivations.

Sports public relations has provided arguably the strongest challenge to professional sports journalism. Sports clubs and organisations have developed their own digital communication channels, known as team media, that have led to the employment of media personnel. Chapter 4 looks at how these team media adopt many of the practices of sports journalism and even employs sports journalists. However, team media are motivated by brand image rather than public service. This chapter also looks at the ways that sports clubs and organisations, in becoming media entities, are increasingly limiting the access of independent sports journalists to athletes and coaches.

Chapter 5 considers the emergence of current or former athletes undertaking sports journalism work, which challenges notions of expertise and objectivity. News organisations are increasingly turning to high-profile 'names' to get their content noticed in the crowded digisphere. This changes the notion of expertise from one in which sports journalists must be observers to one in which 'good' journalism is one that is experiential. It also elevates the concept of 'insider knowledge' to an unbeatable form of access that involves the athlete-journalist being part of the dressing room and professional sport community, as opposed to the outsider-journalist who relies on being granted access. Athlete sports journalism also embraces a subjectivity that places positionality at the heart of the storytelling experience. Athletes have previously taken the role of commenters on the action that augments and complements sports journalism and broadcasting. Athlete sports journalists contribute to the profession by exploring important and insightful areas, such as concussions in football and racism on the field of play.

Chapter 6 focuses on a digital start-up called The Athletic, which has caused significant disruption within US and UK sports journalism. The Athletic is a subscription-based, advertisement-free website that produces local and national sports coverage on both sides of the Atlantic. The Athletic was able to establish instant credibility and legitimacy through its aggressive recruitment strategy of luring many high-profile sports writers away from the mainstream media with big-salary offers, financed by venture capital. The Athletic is also attempting to connect sports journalism to its highly valued practices, such as long-form writing, that have been undermined and threatened by the forces of digital technology. In attempting to be different to the

Introduction 11

mainstream media and establish a clear and distinct market position, The Athletic is experimenting and expanding the boundaries of recognised sports journalism practice in the way that it both covers sports events from outside the press box while conducting interviews and features away from the 'official' sources within professional sport. The Athletic provides a counter-reaction to clickbait culture that has come to define much digital journalism practice. It has instead re-affirmed a commitment to proper and serious sports journalism that is heartening but also loaded with contingency and uncertainty. The Athletic was not yet a profitable business at the time of writing, which means questions still remain regarding its long-term sustainability.

The COVID-19 pandemic has proved to be transformative for journalism's routines in the move to remote ways of working, and these issues are discussed in Chapter 7. However, it presented an unprecedented challenge for sports journalism because sport came to a standstill. Sports journalists were instead required to conjure off-diary stories and exercise advanced professional skills that are more commonly associated with their news colleagues. The restart of sport provided journalists with further opportunities to pursue serious sports journalism and boost their credibility through examining the public health and moral implications of the decision. However, the resumption also brought new professional challenges that are situated in digital technology, such as press conferences on Zoom, which have enabled media managers to exert additional control and generate a greater distance between journalists and the sports they cover. At the time of writing, sports journalists experience uncertainty about whether their already limited access to professional sport will emerge from the pandemic in even worse shape than when it entered.

2 Digital sports journalism

Sports journalism practice has, in common with the wider newsroom, been significantly disrupted by digital technology. Sports journalism is still organised according to a beat system whereby reporters are assigned to teams, regions or sports and conduct field work, in attending both sports events and press conferences. Sports journalists' jobs used to be simply to research, gather and produce stories but, in the digital age, "their work is unable to speak for itself" (Lowes & Robillard, 2018, p. 314). The intensification of both production and consumption dictates that

> in an age of 24/7 media output, and rolling deadlines, the "always on" journalist covering sport has also to be a blogger, a tweeter, and be able to file (or upload) copy for a range of platforms (print, online, mobile).
>
> (Boyle, 2013, p. 92)

Moritz (2015) interviewed one US sports journalist who revealed he was "writing 10–12 traditional stories per week, writing about five blog posts per day, and keeping a constant, active presence on Twitter" (p. 403). Sports journalists also operate in a shared digital environment alongside general users, which means they need to stand out from the crowd (McEnnis, 2013). This loss of monopoly control means that sports journalists' professional standards and distinctiveness are closely scrutinised.

Meanwhile, sports journalism, as an occupational group, has expanded to include new role orientations, platforms, practices, forms and styles as media companies have re-organised and restructured newsrooms in the adaptation to digital media. There are now two broad typologies of sports journalist – the traditional and digitally native (McEnnis, 2020). Role orientations can no longer be seen along

DOI: 10.4324/9781003106869-2

simplistic "print-versus-online terms" (Moritz, 2015, p. 403) because nearly all sports journalism must engage with digital and social media in some shape or form. However, there is a clear division of labour between a traditional journalist, whose core practices and routines – such as mining stories from the professional sport environment – are relatively unchanged, and a digitally native journalist, whose work experience takes place within information technology. This chapter considers what these shifts mean for sports journalism professionalism.

Digital disruption to traditional practice

Sports journalists experienced professional angst in the early transition to the internet, with these feelings being particularly acute for older members of the occupational community (Daum & Scherer, 2018; McGuire & Murray, 2014; Sherwood & Nicholson, 2013). Younger sports journalists, with less entrenched work habits, have been better suited to the agility and flexibility needed to cope with such rapid change, particularly as digital technology evolved quickly at the start of the 21st century. These shifts to more intensive multimedia and multi-platform work demands have required more energy from practitioners as, "whether it is a story, blog post, tweet, or video clip ... reporters ... are being asked to produce much more content than they were even a decade ago" (Moritz, 2015, p. 403). When they are not attending press conferences and sports events, journalists are offering views and opinion through blogs, podcasts and other media appearances. Moritz (2015) notes that "during games and between games, reporters are constantly being asked to create content, filing stories not on a set daily deadline but throughout the day" (p. 404). Sports journalists also feel compelled to tweet and engage with audiences even on days off and while watching sports events at home on television (McEnnis, 2013). At a time when more content needs to be produced to service digital platforms, fewer journalists are involved in this process due to shrinking newsrooms caused by lay-offs. Further, the consolidation of the media, such as the mergers of daily and weekly Sunday staff in the UK national press, have also meant that one sports journalist is performing what used to be the work of two reporters working for separate titles.

The changes in sports journalists' routines speak to two notions of professionalism – occupational and organisational (Aldridge & Evetts, 2003; Ornebring, 2009). Occupational professionalism relates to how practitioners justify their own behaviour through their codes, values, norms and beliefs. Organisational professionalism refers to the way in which employers use these principles to exploit journalists, mainly through altering their work conditions. Here, journalists have an innate sense that they need to bring the news to the public, regardless of the personal risks and sacrifices involved. Journalism contains an 'occupational mythology' that involves editors who intimidate, bully and threaten to replace their journalists at a moment's notice, thus leading to an expectation that new practices and routines are met with little resistance (Aldridge, 1998; Aldridge & Evetts, 2003). News organisations have used digital technology to accentuate these labour issues further, which has been a source of immense stress among sports journalists. Sports journalists have not received any improvement in their pay as they are inhibited from addressing these changes due to the economic precarity of the news business, which has created a fear of job losses (McGuire & Murray, 2016).

The intensification of sports journalism practice has also prompted anxiety over whether high professional standards can be met under such conditions. Sports journalists' ability to produce serious news work is rendered more challenging in a 24/7 cycle of constant news production. Daum and Scherer (2018) argue that "the expansion of the length of the working day only contributes to the erosion of human labour power, the very source of surplus value for capital and the ability of sports journalists to produce quality sports content" (p. 558). Sports journalists struggle to elevate their practice as it is difficult to "obtain the considerable resources and time needed for in-depth investigations into sly practice and systematic corruption" (Hutchins & Boyle, 2017, p. 499). Sports journalists delve further into opinion and subjectivity on social media (Sheffer & Schultz, 2010), while soft news production is more prevalent than hard news on digital platforms (Daum & Scherer, 2018; Lowes & Robillard, 2018). Online audiences tend to engage with news in fleeting and transient ways in online settings, which have led to shorter stories that offer little room to properly contextualise events. This focus on shorter articles has been at the expense of more "in-depth feature articles that once required greater legwork" (Daum & Scherer, 2018, p. 560). News organisations prioritise entertainment values on digital platforms in the pursuit of clicks, which leads to greater emphasis on gossip and rumours. Sports journalists also consider that the quality of their work has suffered because they are spread too thinly across multiple platforms. Sports journalists now have "less time spent reporting the story and more time putting it out across platforms, whether on the Web or tweeting something about it" (McGuire & Murray, 2016, p. 66). Further, sports journalists are now "regularly marketing their stories online, especially on social media"

(Daum & Scherer, 2018, p. 557), which requires added time, energy and emphasis away from the act of story gathering.

New ethical considerations have emerged that are contributing to professional uncertainty. Sports journalists operate in a culture of speed that has prompted concerns over accuracy and fact-checking (English, 2011). This rush to publish has caused changes in how stories are checked prior to publication or broadcast. Then-Sky Sports News executive editor Andy Cairns told a conference in 2018 that the UK 24-hour rolling news channel now makes calculations on the reliability of a single source rather than the previous practice of double sourcing to corroborate information (Bradshaw & Minogue, 2020). Modern practice has also led to pressure on sports journalists to file similar stories from the field. Sugden and Tomlinson (2007) note sports journalists have always limited and restricted news output to ensure that, as competitor-colleagues, they did not scoop each other for fear of incurring the wrath of newsroom managers. Sports journalists are experiencing increasingly restricted access to professional sport, which is further limiting the information available (see Chapter 4: Sports public relations). The commercial focus on hits and page impressions has not only inhibited serious reporting but has also led to more concentrated and similar stories (Cable & Mottershead, 2018). A research interview with a UK sports journalist revealed that he was asked by the online desk to provide them only with stories from Europe's biggest football clubs from Euro 2018 because they generated the most hits (McEnnis, 2018b). The sports journalist also expressed concerns that the pursuit of clicks meant a disregard for the truth, as "… a story that says 'Manchester United are interested in such-and-such', may or may not be true but it has got a quarter-of-a-million views" (McEnnis, 2018b, p. 214).

This homogenisation of media coverage also means that coverage is increasingly narrowed to hyper-commodified sport, such as the UK's Premier League and the US major leagues and, more specifically, to the wealthiest and most globally popular clubs. It also renders coverage of women's sport less likely. Daum and Scherer's (2018) interviews with US sports reporters revealed an industry belief that "women's sport simply cannot deliver a profitable digital audience commodity" (p. 561). Ramon and Tulloch (2019) point out that "the information overload on male professional leagues and international mega-events frequently overlooks lower leagues, youth competitions, and women's games" (p. 3). The regional press has also been criticised for disenfranchising local sport in the pursuit of clicks as it increasingly features national stories. This is the result of an "expansive digital competition for page views, as opposed to an earlier era in which the main competition for a decidedly local audience commodity was once a rival local paper" (Daum & Scherer, 2018, p. 554). For instance, in 2018, Gloucestershire Live in the UK ran a live blog on the sacking of manager Jose Mourinho at Manchester United, a football club around 130 miles away. The editorial decision was justified by the Gloucestershire Live Twitter account as "hard-working journalists seeking new ways to engage with people" (Sharman, 2018). As coverage has consolidated, news organisations are making more calculated and careful decisions on whether to send journalists to sports events on a cost-effective basis. For instance, county cricket in England has seen a decline in sports journalists covering matches with news organisations often content to simply source agency copy at the close of play. The late British sports journalist Martin Johnson lamented that "in the 1980s you needed to get to the ground early to bag a seat in the press box, and earlier still if you wanted to bag the plum positions", but now, "the decline of newspaper cricket coverage for domestic matches means press boxes are nothing like as well occupied as they once were" (Johnson, 2018).

Social and digital media have created professional tensions over who should be breaking sports news stories and how. Sports journalists cultivate their individual profile on social media, which has led to a clash of organisational and individualistic goals and a negotiation of personal and professional identity (Bossio & Sacco, 2016). Journalists tweeting breaking news from their personal accounts is a source of tension with news editors, who would rather utilise official platforms and are concerned that under-cooked stories are made public too early as journalists pursue cultural kudos and more followers (McEnnis, 2021a). News organisations are also pre-occupied with how to present and package stories across digital platforms with one of the central dilemmas being whether they should prioritise analogue or digital platforms. Careful decisions need to be made on whether to hold exclusives back for next-day newspapers or publish web-first. English (2011) finds a mixed picture, with Australian sports journalists tending to adopt a newspaper-orientated approach while in the UK it's more web-first. Broadcast sports journalism faces a similar dilemma in assessing whether to break stories on its television channels or digital platforms (Tomlinson, 2016).

News organisations now expect sports journalists to engage and interact with audiences to foster engagement and build loyalty to the news product. Sports journalists can now develop a dialogue with fans over social media and in below-the-line comments to web stories. However, the shifting emphasis away from control to open participation is problematic for a profession that considers its relationship with readers to be based on a hierarchy of knowledge and a top-down sense of expertise in which stories are 'handed down' and disseminated for informational purposes that require passive consumption (Lewis, 2012). This is particularly the case for sports whereby journalistic discourses of expertise are inextricably linked with insider access and the notion of being an eyewitness and observer of events behind the scenes that fans are excluded from. Sherwood and Nicholson (2013) note that sports journalists "still see themselves as gatekeepers – or the expert that decides what is news and if it is disseminated to the public" (p. 954), although Lowes and Robillard (2018) have called for them to "stop pining for the glory days of being the gatekeepers and the only mediators of sport" now that fans can "publish and circulate their own spectator observations of sporting events, as well as commentary" (p. 316). Sports journalists consider fan forums to be a research tool in "gauging the opinion and reaction of fans" but refuse to acknowledge them as a source (Sherwood & Nicholson, 2013, p. 952). This finding demonstrates the struggles that the profession has in recognising the audience's views as legitimate. Democratic and inclusive approaches to the audience relationship require reversing traditional media understandings of fans that have accumulated over previous decades. Sports fans are represented in the media as emotional, irrational and unbalanced people who have taken to an "obsessive checking of the latest scores" in the Web 2.0 era (Wenner, 2011, p. 71). Further, the inclusion of fans in stories tends to be restricted to vox pops and other items that highlight the irrationality and myopia of fans' passions for their team, which contrasts with the presentation of journalism as controlled, disciplined, steely, calm and objective.

Certainly, the dynamics of social media help to reinforce these hierarchies between sports journalists and fans rather than flatten them. Sports journalists' tweets provide centrepieces whereby they can highlight subjects considered to be of importance. A discussion ensues around that post in the form of replies and this, in turn, can lead to trending topics on Twitter. Here, sports journalists are mobilising their followers in a manner that is not so much about interaction and dialogue but setting the discussion agenda. Social media audiences also realise their own posts and comments acquire greater traction and visibility if they are in reply to the sports journalists' original tweet rather than as a standalone, isolated post. Sports journalists therefore cementing their authority as the initial tweet is of primary significance and the ensuing replies are secondary and reactive.

Twitter also provides sports journalists with a platform to emphasise the importance of their work to others, which augments their core production. Sports journalists often record Twitter and Facebook Lives of themselves using their mobile phones while out in the field, which trades on the public perception that their jobs are glamorous and desirable. These emergent practices draw attention to sports journalists' insider access and serve to remind audiences of this privilege. The videos offer insights into the experience of travelling to assignments and providing 'behind-the-scenes' footage of reporting from press boxes. Sports journalists relay team news or other insights from the sports arena by talking directly into the cameras on their mobile phones. Sports journalists are omnipresent in the digital age to remind audiences of who they are, what they do and the importance and significance of their news work. However, the reality behind beat sports journalism is one of dwindling glamour and desirability as its practitioners feel the squeeze of the business pressures of news media. Even leading sportswriters have seen their lavish treatment in overseas assignments diminish. GQ magazine quoted a sportswriter as saying: "I know a couple who stay in Travelodges now. One of them told me it was like Death of A Salesman" (Franklin-Wallis, 2020).

The emergence of the digital sports journalist

News organisations have restructured newsrooms to service multiple platforms, which has led to the creation of digitally specific roles. There are, however, clear distinctions between traditional and digital sports journalists. For instance, *The Times* chief football writer Henry Winter, considered to be one of the leading sports journalists in the UK, would not be expected to run a live blog with blow-by-blow updates of the sports event. However, this restructuring of newsrooms, while primarily driven by commercial factors, has created a fragmented and disparate professional group. These digitally native roles have adopted new approaches and routines that challenge and conflict with historical understandings of sports journalism.

Managers have imposed digitally native journalism on the newsroom, which means that its practitioners still need to achieve legitimation and acceptance within the wider occupational community (McEnnis, 2020). Digital sports journalists are organised in ways that enable them to produce content quickly and cheaply. Unlike traditional role holders, they are not posted to arenas and stadiums around the world but instead cover sport from the office using the mediated experience of live television broadcasts of the spectacle. Digitally native sports journalism therefore tends to be office-based and places emphasis on sourcing stories from the web. It can involve gathering strands of digital communication from elsewhere on the internet, such as YouTube videos, tweets, Instagram posts and other user-generated content. Digitally native sports journalism often involves curation and moderation of second-hand material. These routines can also include repurposing and repackaging stories produced by traditional sports journalists across different platforms as news organisations seek to find different ways to connect and engage with fragmented audiences.

Digital sports journalism also approaches social media as fertile ground for news generation. Twitter and Instagram feed journalists with unfiltered comments from athletes that they would not be able to source from more sanitised and stage-managed press conferences and briefings. Hutchins and Rowe (2012), in invoking the French philosopher Paul Virilio, describe these faux pas as "information accidents" (p. 72) that provide juicy stories for sports desks, with the subsequent reactions of governing bodies providing good follow-up material. An example of an 'information accident' is Manchester United striker Edinson Cavani including a racial slur in a post that thanked a follower for congratulating him on a performance against Southampton in 2020. Consequently, Cavani was banned for three matches and fined £100,000 by the Football Association (Rathborn, 2020). However, sourcing stories from social media is also considered to be a form of 'low' journalism that raises ethical issues. Sports journalists must be certain that an athlete's account is genuine. An example comes from 2019 when ESPN SportsCenter inadvertently reported on a fake Instagram account posing as Los Angeles Lakers basketball superstar LeBron James appearing to comment on trade rumours involving New Orleans Pelicans player Anthony Davis, who had been linked with a move to the Lakers. ESPN's response to being tricked was to condemn the faker rather than admit to their own professional failings by stating that the post was made "by some kid with way too much time on his hands" (Heck, 2019). However, the bypassing of traditional media also means that athletes avoid scrutiny from journalists and can set their own agenda.

However, these routines are unrecognisable with how sports journalism has always seen itself. Here, the emphasis has been on field work, being out of the office and on the road, and developing human contacts and relationships within professional sport in the pursuit of stories. Traditional sports journalists are concerned that these emerging practices undermine their arguments about what constitutes their professional distinctiveness in the digital age (McEnnis, 2020). Traditional sports journalists also use their digital colleagues as a discursive strategy to emphasise that their accreditation to professional sport and attendance at events are acts of proper and genuine sports journalism (McEnnis, 2020). Legacy, newspaper-based practices are still considered within newsroom culture to be of over-arching importance even though news organisations are placing increasing emphasis – and resources – on digital production. Digital sports journalists are further de-legitimised by the removal of 'journalist' from their job titles. These roles are instead often referred to as 'content providers'. For Daum and Scherer (2018), "the shift in professional title is not only pejorative but also emblematic of a corporate-wide policy of digital quantity over professional quality" (p. 558). Their professional standing is not helped by the terms in which digital sports journalists are recruited. Online sports journalism roles have increased as news organisations attempt to publish across multiple digital platforms to reach a highly fragmented audience. The labour arrangements tend to be casualised and low paid. Digital sports journalism's positioning within the journalism labour market does nothing for its occupational status and is a far cry from the more vaunted end of journalism where an elite few are handsomely rewarded with six-figure salaries (Boyle, 2006). Digital positions often recruit younger sports journalists, usually graduates, and there are questions as to whether these practices meet their professional expectations and ambitions of working in the industry.

Digital sports journalism: Innovation or churnalism?

Sports journalists have developed a reputation for innovation despite the confusion, insecurity and uncertainty that they are experiencing in the digital age. Morrison (2014) argues the toy department reputation has worked in sports journalism's favour because it created a nothing-to-lose attitude when it came to experimentation. *The New York Times* sports desk effectively created the multimedia long-form storytelling experience, which has been widely adopted by the news media. "Snow Fall: The Avalanche at Tunnel Creek", about a team of leading US skiers and snowboarders whose trip to the Cascade Mountains in Washington state ended in tragedy, won the *New York Times* a Pulitzer Prize in Feature Writing in 2013 as a groundbreaking and influential approach to long-form storytelling on digital platforms. In doing so, the *New York Times* resolved the issue of how to deliver lengthy, in-depth storytelling on a digital platform in a manner that could keep audiences engaged, involving "graphics, animation and video" (Dowling & Vogan, 2015, p. 213). The phrase 'can we "snowfall" this?' has become part of newsroom vernacular in assessing whether a story deserves the long-form multimedia treatment (Dowling & Vogan, 2015). Snow Fall's influence and legacy have grown since as developments in digital technology, such as the software package Shorthand, have made multimedia storytelling cheaper and easier to produce.

Another key example of sports journalism innovation is live blogging, now a widespread and prominent digital format (McEnnis, 2016; Thurman & Walters, 2013). Live blogging involves journalists aligning themselves with fans through the shared experience of watching sports events on television (McEnnis, 2016). It also sees sports journalists present themselves not only as providers of information but as mediators of conversation with audiences. Morrison (2014) notes sports journalism is perfectly suited to a digital environment in the way it generates plentiful discussion points that can provide the basis for the development of online communities with audiences. Live blogs constitute an inclusive form of journalistic practice in the way that debate is stimulated and audience comments are published. This move to greater informality and conversation by sports journalists is in contrast to the formalities and strict conventions of beat journalism. Kroon and Eriksson (2019) note that this greater informality is also present in the broadcast industry, where presenters who usually wear formal dress, such as suits on television, and read pre-written scripts on television are allowed to wear casual dress and ad-lib on web video shows. Kroon and Eriksson (2019) discovered that as sports journalists have moved into digital spaces they have become more informal and amateurish, leading to greater sports talk. Kroon and Eriksson (2019) analysed three Swedish webcasts produced by mainstream media organisations and found there was a "more relaxed and spontaneous tone in online sports talk" (p. 844). This study connects well with Carlson's (2015) notion of journalistic expansion whereby journalists extend the boundaries of acceptable linguistic and structural norms. Yet traditional media spaces, such as newspapers and television, have retained their formal codes, language and practices even when surrounded by digital communication, suggesting that the boundaries of professional acceptability vary according to medium.

Sports journalism's fixation with data and statistics lends itself to the use of interactive graphics and data visualisation (Morrison, 2014). Rojas-Torrijos (2020) argues that sports journalism's use of gamification, far from being a gimmick, actually plays a crucial role in helping audiences to understand the complexities and context surrounding sport. Social and digital media can also be empowering for more marginalised voices within sports journalism. For instance, in the UK, the Offside Rule Podcast, named after a typically sexist comment to female football fans, is hosted by three women sports journalists, Lynsey Hooper, Hayley McQueen and Kait Borsay. However, there is a counter-argument to these innovative practices. Multimedia storytelling experiences such as Snow Fall are occasional forays that do not define most online stories and the day-to-day lived experience of digital journalists. Live blogging, for all its inclusiveness and shared fan experience, is ultimately sourcing and collating second-hand information across media, and is still reliant on the work of traditional journalists in providing first-hand newsgathering and the fact-checking and verification with human sources that this entails. Daum and Scherer (2018) argue that the "emphasis on statistics and short analytical pieces to drive page views … has only further marginalized the already minimal presence of in-depth coverage of social issues in sport" (p. 565).

The promise of building constructive online communities does not quite match the reality. Instead, sports journalists have to deal with substantial social media abuse and antagonism from users (McEnnis, 2021a; Sharman, 2020). Sky Sports in the UK considered social media abuse to be such an extensive problem facing its sports journalists that it launched a "Unite Against Online Hate and Abuse" campaign (Sky Sports, 2021a). This abuse is also racialised and gendered, with one black male journalist describing how he had banana and gorilla emojis sent to him, while one female journalist was told that she looked ugly without make-up. Although social and digital media provide a platform for gender empowerment, all too often this is in response to discriminatory and criminal behaviour experienced by women in their occupational routines. Female sports journalists in Brazil were compelled to launch an anti-harassment campaign with the hashtag #DeixaElaTrabalhar ("Let Her Do Her Job"), raising awareness of the fact that they were being sexually and verbally assaulted (Downie, 2018).

Digital sports journalism, in common with the wider newsroom, can also involve looser professional practices and clickbait content in the servicing of a digital business model of clicks, hits and bounce rates. Ramon and Tulloch (2019) argue that "the progressive shift towards provocative, entertaining and clickbait-oriented content seems to define how a large amount of sports news is currently being manufactured and packaged" (p. 3). Hutchins and Rowe (2012) use the concept of "creative cannibalization" (p. 141) in asserting that, while journalism and plagiarism is an issue that has always existed, it has been accentuated and become more shameless in the digital age. The speed and ease of information flows provides opportunities for sports sites to re-direct the traffic for that story to their site, away from their rivals where the story originated. This copying culture also leads to a decline in professional standards towards verification and accuracy in that digital sports journalists are not strictly relying on their own checks. Digital sports journalists also make emphatic use of wire services, such as Press Association, Associated Press and Reuters, as they service a limitless digital space that core staffing and resources cannot fully cover (Lange, Nicholson & Hess, 2007). This move, alongside the focus on the same teams and the same sports discussed earlier in the chapter, contributes to the homogeneity of content. English's (2014) analysis of web sports content across Australia, India and the UK broadsheet news organisations found that it contained significant amounts of material like that produced by domestic rivals and relatively few examples of articles containing exclusive information. This was often in contrast to the comments of most sports journalists, who considered their content to be different from that of rivals.

Conclusion

Sports journalism has lost its monopoly on content and communication in the digital age and must instead convince audiences of its continuing relevance, distinctiveness and significance. Social and digital media provide traditional sports journalists with the opportunity to engage in discursive strategies that draw attention to their historical marker of expertise, access and accreditation to the live sports event, using tweets, YouTube videos, Twitter/Facebook Lives and podcasts. Sports journalists continue to trade on their accreditation to professional sport as vital to providing them with valuable 'insider information' that makes them worth following on social media. Journalists position themselves as centrepieces around which sports discussion can take place, which helps to maintain their authority. Journalists are also able to build on the glamour and desirability of their jobs through publishing videos and photographs of themselves at sports events.

However, this strident confidence conceals a fragility, insecurity and concern over professional standards and the ability to conduct serious news work. The proliferation of sports podcasts and intensive social media use encourages greater subjectivity and opinion. These developments within sports journalism are consistent with a general newsroom shift to more emotive, commentary-based, subjective journalism on social media (Wahl-Jorgensen, 2016). Moritz (2015) makes the important point that journalists' professional norms and values have not changed from the analogue age, but "their day-to-day work routines are where the most change appears to be happening" (p. 407). Sports journalists are essentially performing similar tasks to the pre-digital age of attending sports events and press conferences, but they must also produce more content around these activities to service multiple digital platforms, which can provide a distraction from serious newsgathering.

Meanwhile, metrics-driven editorial decision making is leading to shorter, less in-depth pieces that mean sports journalists are unable to properly contextualise and explain the issues they are writing about. They also must curate social media accounts while promoting and marketing their own work. These highly intensive activities lead to mental and physical burnout among sports journalists (Daum & Scherer, 2018), which renders serious news work, and the substantive amounts of both time and energy required, a distant ambition. For Daum and Scherer (2018), the organisational focus on skillsets that involve producing "even greater amounts of daily digital content, including the creation of audio and video features ... have very little to do with the craft of journalism" (p. 557). Further, the re-organisation of sports desks to service digital platforms has led to proper journalism becoming a specific and specialist activity that is held by employees with titles such as 'sports news reporter'. Certainly, the days when serious news work was a general expectation among practitioners appear to be over.

Sports journalism, then, has become a sprawling occupation of myriad role orientations with their own routines, practices and interpretations of occupational ideology. Many of these positions no longer adhere to historical beliefs, codes and values of practice, which lead to internal tensions and boundary contests. Traditional sports journalists still consider themselves to be providing society with news and information from professional sport, whereas digitally native sports journalists perceive audience engagement and community building to be a public service. However, digital news work is still seen within the occupational culture as rather lowly (McEnnis, 2020) and this is reflected in the pay, conditions and description of 'content providers', which removes any responsibility for producing proper journalism (Daum & Scherer, 2018).

Digital sports journalists are likely to continue to expand in number as news organisations increasingly focus on their online platforms. News organisations realise that positioning these as graduate-entry roles enables them to suppress pay and conditions while the news work that they produce, such as live blogs, requires few resources. For cash-strapped news organisations seeking to produce more with less, it is hardly surprising that digital sports journalism is seen as a more financially viable proposition than the more costly traditional sports journalist, who requires much greater resources in terms of travel and accommodation for attending sports events. The end result could well be the de-professionalisation of sports journalism. This de-professionalisation is likely to be accentuated further as automated sports journalism becomes increasingly prevalent in newsrooms in the coming years. Automation has heightened the tensions within sports journalism between the traditional hermeneutic, human-oriented storytelling and the increasing move to 'cold and clinical' digital technology-driven statistics, data and quantitative information. As Miller (2021) argues, "think of the 'expected goals' category that almost trumps, you know, goals scored" (p. 372). Sports journalism's propensity for statistics and data and formulaic writing practices such as match reporting makes it fertile ground for automation (Galily, 2018; Rojas-Torrijos & Toural Bran, 2019). The vast churn and turnover of sports stories on digital platforms would justify the high training and development costs of robots (Galily, 2018). Automated sports journalism also requires additional resources to pay third-party data and automation companies to provide the technical expertise and the information service. This means that budgets could be further directed away from funding serious sports journalism. For example, Associated Press has combined data from Sportradar and automation technology from Data Skrive to produce text previews of Major League Soccer (MLS) matches. Associated Press utilises another third-party automation company, Automated Insights, to produce previews and recaps of men's college basketball games (Associated Press, 2019). News organisations have also started directly using automated technology. For instance, *The Washington Post* developed an automated storytelling bot to cover the 2016 Summer Olympics and 2018 Winter Olympics (Rojas-Torrijos, 2019).

The continued development of automated technology will undoubtedly lead to further consolidation, shrinkage and lay-offs of sports journalists, and the creation of new, low-skilled, low-paid newsroom roles that interface with the automatically produced stories. In the hands of media corporates, it is difficult to see the primary considerations as anything other than cutting costs and producing content as cheaply as possible. Kunert (2020) argues that software and data providers of automated sports journalism might even "turn from *implicit* to *explicit* interlopers, which feature their own media coverage and then do challenge journalistic authority, similar to blogs and citizen journalists" (p. 13). However, there could be some advantages to automated developments, such as allowing sports journalists to focus on more human-interest and empathy-driven stories. Galily (2018) notes that, "Paradoxically, rapidly growing automated technology has highlighted the human advantage of telling the story in the sporting world" (p. 50), while Kunert (2020) couches this greater freedom in terms of "more time for interviews and other exclusive stories" (p. 13). Inevitably, though, it will involve fewer sports journalists performing these tasks.

3 Sports blogging

A significant disruption for sports journalists in the digital age is that they are now one of many actors in the mass communication process (Boyle, 2013). A proliferation of fan-produced sports media has emerged in the digital age as websites, blogs, podcasts and video channels have become an integral part in the digital information ecosystem. Here, fans have adopted the practices, styles and forms that we historically associate with professional sports journalism. News, opinions, interviews and podcasts are common features of sports journalism yet they are also produced by fans themselves. These developments have called into question sports journalists' professional distinctiveness and their authority and privilege – issues that used to be taken for granted in an analogue era of monopoly control. Broader shifts in the sports media industry over the past 30 years, particularly the expansion of pay-TV, have meant audiences can now watch mediated live sports events and are therefore not as reliant on sports journalists as 'eye-witnesses'. This places fans in a position where they can report, analyse and comment on the sporting spectacle, which means that "the differences between sports journalists and spectator content producers are diminishing" (Lowes & Robillard, 2018, p. 311).

This chapter focuses on aspects of the blogosphere that have significance for sports journalism. Previous research has found that bloggers can be motivated by simply the love of writing or the need to build community among a select group of people, with no aspirations to develop substantive audiences or professionalise either themselves or the activity (McCarthy, 2013, 2014). However, other studies have revealed that sports journalists should be worried, with Daum and Scherer (2018) describing bloggers as "credible competitors to the writing of sports journalists" (p. 554). Sports bloggers can also be seen as a response to sports journalism's 'toy department' shortcomings in the way that they are "taking on the responsibilities of sport journalists to carry out the mediation of their sport in ways they perceive to be lacking in mainstream sport-news coverage" (Lowes &

DOI: 10.4324/9781003106869-3

Robillard, 2018, p. 313). Sports bloggers can be keen to avoid the 'sports journalist' tag for fear of being associated with the lowly reputation that comes with it, even though they see themselves as producing sports journalism (Kian, Burden & Shaw, 2011).

This analysis begins by looking at how sports bloggers are addressing the perceived failures of sports journalism. The case of Deadspin, in the US, has drawn scholarly attention for the way it eschews the access of sports journalism and the ethical conflicts that this presents by taking a more distanced approach to sports coverage. Further, sports blogging can counter the mainstream media by challenging dominant framings and addressing absences in coverage, such as marginalised groups or sports. Sports blogging is therefore more than just being a 'fan with a notebook'. These developments exert pressure on sports journalists to justify themselves while highlighting their inadequacies and holding them accountable for whether they are sufficiently engaging in serious news work.

Sports journalists have also been confronted with news organisations' realisation of blogging's potential to provide cheap content and labour for their digital platforms. Therefore, sports journalism must carefully manage the inclusion of bloggers and blogging in professional spaces. One of the key projects in this respect has been the Guardian Sports Network in the UK, where bloggers are incorporated under a philosophy of 'open journalism' yet are cordoned into a very specific area of the website and are mobilised by professional journalists. Further, sports media companies, in their quest to attract younger audiences, wish to tap into the zeitgeist of blogging's cultural cache. The case of US blogger Grantland Rice and media giant ESPN joining forces on an ill-fated project called Grantland reveals many of the tensions and issues that exist in this rather uncomfortable relationship.

The chapter then progresses to the discursive response of sports journalists in maintaining their territory of accreditation in official sports. Far from encouraging sports journalism to think more widely about its coverage, sports journalists have doubled down on their physical boundary markers within professional sport. Sports journalists also establish a presence in the sports blogosphere, which, far from establishing inclusivity and openness, draws attention to the special, authoritative position of sports journalists as experts and reminds audiences of their distinction from fans.

Blogging as alternative sports journalism

It is worth noting at this stage that these developments are not exclusive to digital platforms but can still be found in old media, where alternative media producers like to call upon analogue platforms as markers of quality, longevity and respect. Ramon and Tulloch (2019) draw attention to the rise of an independent sports magazine market that offers resistance to narrow news agendas and celebritised media narratives. Here, the independent sports magazine market sets out to "explore the social, political, cultural and economic ramifications of sports" (p. 4) and is motivated by both "a disenchantment with routine football journalism" (p. 9) and a "reaction to fast-food sports journalism" (p. 11). One participant, Anders Bengtsson, of Swedish magazine *Offside*, lamented, "how many stories can one write about (Swedish footballer) Zlatan Ibrahimovic?" (p. 9).

While digital platforms can be associated with dumbed-down and transient forms of sports journalism, they can also provide an edginess, subversiveness, irascibility and informality that is not encumbered by centuries of the print tradition. Blogs that seek to fill the void created by sports journalism's perceived failings can take a deliberately oppositional and confrontational tone to mainstream media. Here, bloggers tap into the mistrust towards sports journalism and play on suspicions that their loyalties lie with the professional sport corporate machine rather than the interests of the average fan. One of the more high-profile and successful sports blogs in this regard is the US website Deadspin. Deadspin has attracted attention from the academy for being a form of "interloper media" (Eldridge, 2018, pp. 857–858) that has adopted the subversive spirit of punk culture (Serazio, 2021).

Deadspin was founded in 2005 by Will Leitch, who later became a writer for New York magazine and mlb.com, among others, and is currently part of G/O Media. Deadspin adopts an 'anti-establishment' position through its 'anti-accreditation' stance in rejecting sports journalism's access to professional sport. Deadspin's tagline of "sports news without fear, favour or compromise" is a clear broadside at journalists for their perceived ethical failings. Deadspin is clearly aligning itself with fans who have been alienated, disenchanted and disenfranchised from the hyper-commodified professional sport environment in which they are now customers rather than citizens. Deadspin does not threaten the journalistic haven of accreditation to professional sport, but it demonstrates that good journalism can be performed outside of it and challenges professional sports journalism for its obsession with official sources. Serazio (2021) notes that access was considered a liability, with Deadspin fearing "they'd start experiencing sports differently from the average fan; start writing for others inside the press box; start compromising because of compromising arrangements" (p. 6).

Deadspin therefore sees the ability to hold power to account as not being located inside sports but outside. Serazio (2021) argues that Deadspin "see themselves as the *true* inheritors of the Fourth Estate, watchdogging in the public interest, and oriented toward power more critically than their lackey counterparts in the mainstream commercial media" (p. 4). Here, professionalism is not the key to exiting the toy department but a subversive, maverick approach to journalism. It is the role of outsider and outlier, on the social margins – an active rejection of professionalism and the conformity that comes with it – that is the path to journalistic credibility. Deadspin connects with the more experimental strand of sports journalism's history, such as Hunter S. Thompson's Gonzo journalism and the rejection of the objectivity norm (Serazio, 2021). Deadspin is a modern reworking of a subversive position that asserts that to hold sport to account, you must step out of its power structures. The key to independence and autonomy is not within professionalism and its commercial conflicts but outside of it. For Deadspin, "cultural authority derives from the *absence* of establishment qualifications" (Serazio, 2021, p. 10).

Deadspin instead encourages tip-offs from fans and launches its own investigations. Deadspin often turns its ire towards the mainstream media and considers journalists, in being part of the sports-media complex, to be embedded within corporate power structures and interests. Sports journalism needs scrutinising and holding to account as well, with ESPN attracting particularly strong criticism (Burroughs & Vogan, 2015; Serazio, 2021). Sports journalists know that any deviation from professional standards will be excoriated on the Deadspin site. One of the more famous stories that Deadspin has broken, the Manti-Te'o fiasco, was the result of reporters Timothy Burke and Jack Dickey investigating an anonymous tip that the American footballer's claim his girlfriend had leukaemia was not genuine. They found Te'o had been the victim of a 'catfish scam' in which what he thought was an online relationship with 'Lenny Kekua' was a hoax (Burke & Dickey, 2013). This significant breaking story enabled Deadspin to conduct vital boundary work that attempted to convince audiences its subversive approach achieved results and "the interlopers were doing the real journalistic work" (Serazio, 2021, p. 8). With the Te'o story, Deadspin also positioned itself as "blowing the whistle on negligent fact-checking due diligence" (Serazio, 2021, p. 8) within the mainstream media. For instance, *Sports Illustrated* had failed to check whether Kekua actually existed and published the error in a feature headlined 'The Full Manti', while ESPN hesitated to break the news ahead of Deadspin because it wanted an on-camera interview with Te'o (Burroughs & Vogan, 2015;

Sandomir & Miller, 2013). Video footage of Te'o's response would have performed well commercially and this allowed Deadspin to develop a narrative in which "ESPN's decision evinces the powerful media outlet's tendency to privilege its commercial priorities over its commitment to informing the public" (Burroughs & Vogan, 2015, p. 93). Further, ESPN's desire to corroborate the story with Te'o himself shows the mainstream media's reliance on seeking approval from 'official' sources before running stories and their fear of losing access without it (Yoder, 2013).

Deadspin's wings were eventually clipped when its new owners, Great Hill Partners – a Boston-based private equity firm – told the site to stick to sports and desist venturing into politics (Walsh, 2019). This new editorial strategy clearly failed to understand the 'interloper' role of Deadspin, its historical antecedents and the nature of blogging culture. It led to the interim editor, Barry Petchesky, being fired for not conforming to the new policy and six other staff resignations, including leading reporter Megan Greenwell (Bauder, 2019). Serazio (2021) argues that the muzzling and restraining of Deadspin mirrors the trajectory of punk in that "it got chewed up and spit out, but left a legacy internalized there with its style, skepticism, and subjectivity of coverage" (p. 14).

Another challenge to mainstream media approaches and narratives can be found in bloggers who advance social justice causes. Blogging practices can even be seen in a rejection of the hierarchy of mainstream media in the way that they are often democratic and collaborative among particular sport communities (McCarthy, 2012). Blogging is not necessarily a subversive practice and can take its cues from mainstream media. Sports journalists can provide a source of stories to which bloggers then react (McCarthy, 2012). Vimieiro (2018) notes that one of the benefits of the blogosphere is placing supporters at the heart of stories. In analysing Brazilian fan-produced media, Vimieiro (2018) found that "in the centre of the narratives, we find the supporters, not players and football leaders" (p. 384). The author points to a 'Saint Victor's Day', an annual commemoration by Atletico Mineiro fans of a penalty save from goalkeeper Victor that kept the club in the Copa Libertadores da America competition in 2013 and which they went on to win. Here, the "narratives of the supporters ... accurately express the suffering, pain, agony and redemption they experienced" (Vimieiro, 2018, p. 384).

This fan-focused storytelling contrasts heavily with the mainstream media's obsession with celebrity narratives in professional sport. Bloggers can also bring to the fore under-represented groups and subjects in journalism. Journalism's fixation with male, professional, spectator sport is not always a reflection of how the public wish to engage with and discuss it. For example, Antunovic and Hardin's (2013) study of women bloggers on the *BlogHer* network found they wanted to discuss their own physical activity and provide well-being advice. There has also been interest among academics at how non-mainstream sources of sport media are pursuing an alternative and diverse agenda that is interested in issues of social justice (Forde & Wilson, 2018; Ramon & Tulloch, 2019). Forde and Wilson (2018) found that sports activist blogs take a collaborative approach to working with journalists. RioWatch, a blogging site that raises awareness of the social effects of the 2014 football World Cup and the 2016 Olympics on Rio, "provided support for journalists in terms of connecting them with community members, offering tours and historical context, and providing guides and translators to visiting journalists" (p. 70). Here, bloggers recognise the value of working with sports journalists and accessing their sizeable audiences to raise awareness and effect social change. Such collaborative and co-operative approaches towards professional sports journalism are in marked contrast to more confrontational and oppositional narratives propounded by the likes of Deadspin.

Forde and Wilson (2018) also point to the way social media functionality involves the grouping of posts and articles around a particular topic whereby sports journalists' work sits alongside that of academics and activists. Here, the authors point to writings on the American footballer Colin Kaepernick for his bended-knee protest during the US national anthem being collated under the creation of a #ColinKaepernickSyllabus, which "operates as a living, open-source and collaboratively collated document" (p. 73). So even if sports journalists are not willing to collaborate as they try and protect their professional boundaries, the algorithms and functionality in digital technology may not give them a choice. For sports journalists, working with activists, such as charities, campaign groups and academics, can provide a useful and accessible source alternative to the frustrations that they experience in the professional sport environment. Rowe (2017), in his trenchant criticism of sports journalism's lack of scrutiny over corruption in football's governing body, FIFA, argues that "the full media apparatus from alert, questioning citizens to 'guerrilla,' 'whistle blowing' operations to large media corporations needs to be mobilized to use all available media technologies to enrich the collective representation and knowledge of sport" (p. 527). However, there are a number of barriers to this. There may be a reluctance on the part of sports journalists to write stories that challenge power and privilege in sport because it will invariably upset the day-to-day 'official' sources, such as clubs, organisations and governing bodies, that in some way may contribute to the injustices being railed against. News organisations may also be concerned that such non-celebrity driven narratives will not perform well commercially, particularly in digital settings, by failing to reach sufficient hits and page impressions to attract advertisers.

Sports journalism and acceptable blogging

These potential barriers to collaboration are not to say that sports journalists are reluctant to work with the blogosphere at all. However, sports journalists must carefully negotiate these parameters as news managers recognise the potential for recruiting bloggers as effectively a cheap form of labour. Subsequently, a 'complementary' form of sports blogging has emerged that acts as a supplement to mainstream media coverage (McEnnis, 2017). Here, bloggers pursue niche or quirky subject matter that sits alongside beat reporting. An example here is blogs on football tactics that augment reports and reaction from journalists embedded within professional sport (McEnnis, 2017). Bloggers can also provide a support role in viewing the sports event from the comfort of their armchairs, often in different cities to the teams that they specialise in writing analysis and opinion about (Daum & Scherer, 2018). Previous research has found that bloggers rarely attend sports events they write about (Kian, Burden & Shaw, 2011). These bloggers are not conflicting with sports journalists' core routines and are not seeking to disrupt the accreditation process to professional sport. Digital environments, unlike the spatial restrictions of analogue media, have made unlimited content possible. The use of bloggers by mainstream media has raised questions about digital labour and exploitation. Daum and Scherer (2018), in their study of Canadian media group Postmedia, found that sports journalism has been 'outsourced' to bloggers at cheaper rates than how professionals are employed. Often, these arrangements follow the laying-off of full-time sports journalists and are a substitute for hiring new entrants – what the authors describe as "the new precariat" (p. 561). However, Daum and Scherer (2018) found that, despite poorer pay and conditions to professional sports journalists, bloggers could actually generate more sizeable audiences to their work.

Further, bloggers have been a useful source of labour as news organisations that were previously national now seek trans-national audiences to grow revenue, which means that content needs to have global appeal. Sports journalist Sean Ingle described how *The Guardian* mobilised a network of 150 fans from around the world for the 2010 football World Cup. He stated that: "We knew exactly what it was like in downtown Accra, for example, when Ghana qualified for the quarter-finals because we had people from the Guardian fans' network tweeting and blogging and sending us pictures via Flickr" (*The Guardian*, 2012). News organisations do not have the resources for sports journalists to cover every nation at a global mega-sports environment so bloggers from different countries become critically important in helping to provide this comprehensive coverage.

In such circumstances, sports journalists retain their gatekeeping role as the arbiters of content worth reading or viewing. It excludes sports blogs that are not used by news organisations from the conversation. Sports journalists legitimise these complementary blogs as the best out there and being deserving of mainstream media recognition. *The Guardian* has solidified this arrangement through its sports network, whereby an approved stable of bloggers feed into a clearly demarcated and tagged area of the site. The Guardian Sports Network is, in the main, sports coverage at a distance – away from the access and accreditation of professional sport. Here, *The Guardian* operates a revenue sharing model with the blogger that enables the news organisation to extract advertising revenue from the blogger's labour. The blogger gains exposure and access to a wider audience that links back to the blog. By including blog posts under a separate banner, *The Guardian* is clearly distinguishing between amateur and professional content. Further, *The Guardian* employs a sports community editor to run its sports network that involves establishing a relationship with bloggers, similar to the one that news editors forge with reporters (McEnnis, 2017). Dart (2009) argues that mainstream-media control of bloggers discourages dissenting voices. However, news organisations' attempts to expand coverage by utilising bloggers can give a voice to marginalised voices, reflected in articles on how football remains unwelcoming for gay fans (Hunter, 2020), and other social concerns, such as elitism in English cricket (Wallace, 2020).

Sports bloggers also have a complex relationship with mainstream media. On the one hand, bloggers refuse to identify as journalists because they do not want to be tarnished with the 'toy department' reputation (Kian, Burden & Shaw, 2011). However, they recognise news organisations can give them access to credibility and audiences that help them to grow their personal brand and drive traffic to their website. Vogan and Dowling (2016) chronicle the partnership between the US blogger Bill Simmons and sports media giant ESPN through a vehicle called Grantland. Grantland, which evoked the name of legendary sportswriter Grantland Rice, was a multimedia sports journalism product that connected digital to print, signposting "ideologically constructed meanings that designate certain media as having greater aesthetic worth than others" (p. 25). ESPN could benefit from the cultural kudos of a popular blogger among sports fans while also inserting itself into "sports writing's print heritage ... it has the cultural authority to mediate and even contribute to this rarefied tradition" (p. 32).

Meanwhile, Simmons could self-present as "a product of the genre's heritage and leader of its digital vanguard" (p. 32). He started to reject blogs as "unprofessional and even lawful" (p. 30). Vogan and Dowling (2016) make reference to boundary work when they describe Simmons' assault on online sports media as giving him "the unique authority to decide what counts as legitimate online sports writing ... his responses to blogging and Twitter position him as a vigilant guardian of traditional sports journalism" (p. 30). Vogan and Dowling (2016) make the interesting point that for all his cultural kudos and edginess, in harking back to the literary traditions of sports writing via Grantland he is advocating a "surprisingly conservative media ideology" (p. 30). Nevertheless, Simmons still found himself suspended three times by ESPN for criticising or challenging the network. Eventually, ESPN decided they had had enough and sacked Simmons in 2015, with the closure of Grantland following months later (Manfred, 2015; Sims, 2015).

There are two possible conclusions to draw here. Firstly, the blogger relationship with mainstream media is a paradoxical one that is difficult to reconcile. On the one hand, bloggers want the credibility and recognition that the mainstream media bestows upon them, but their outside and non-conformist attitude clashes with corporate and brand image. Secondly, long-form and quality sports journalism may generate cultural capital but it eventually meets a cold, hard economic reality of big sports media business.

Stay out of the press box: Protecting boundaries from bloggers

Simmons as a disruptive force in sports journalism goes further still. Sports journalists not only share digital communication and social media channels with bloggers, but they can also be colleagues within the same news organisation. How sports journalists manage this arrangement is crucial to maintaining their professional boundaries. Not surprisingly, Simmons was criticised by traditional sports journalists who used, as Leitch (2009) describes, "those tired Doesn't Sit in the Press Box arguments". Leitch (2009) locates an important discursive strategy in sports journalists' boundary work –

the notion that being present at the sports event itself is essential for credibility and authority. In research interviews, sports journalists have defined their professional expertise according to accreditation to professional sport and access to official sources (McEnnis, 2017). This accreditation is generally awarded to mainstream media. Sports journalists therefore know that access is a useful, achievable and clear physical barrier between them and bloggers.

It therefore becomes a problem if bloggers seek to gain access to the press box and accreditation to professional sport. The admission of outsiders into press boxes and briefings challenges sports journalists' professional distinctiveness. In the US, bloggers such as Rivals.com, BleacherReport.com, SBNation.com, 247.com, and Scout.com. request accreditation, "creating questions among sports-communications officers about when and to whom to grant access" (Suggs, 2015, p. 47). Suggs (2016) notes that "there is little transparency or rational evaluation" (p. 270) in the granting of media access, although "traditional patterns of prioritizing national or 'big name' media" (p. 274) are maintained. The concern for sports journalists is that as bloggers continue to become established and accepted in the communication landscape, acquire credibility and attract sizeable audiences, this balance of power may start to shift in the future.

Journalists invoke their professional ideology to justify special status that is also designed at excluding outsiders (McEnnis, 2013, 2017). Journalists perceive bloggers as negatively impacting on their ability to work as a pack and extract newsworthy information from their interviewee. Sports journalists engage in rhetorical boundary work to police the issue of bloggers attending press conferences. Justin Allen, a sports reporter with *The Sun*, referred to bloggers when he stated in a research interview:

> They really mess up your press conferences. They come up with an absolutely ridiculous question. A question that's maybe been answered already, or something that's not in relation to anything … It breaks up the flow of the press conference and the manager might be thinking for a minute about that stupid question they've had and you're trying to ask a proper question.
> (McEnnis, 2017, pp. 557–558)

However, sports journalists consider bloggers who attend press conferences but do not ask questions as benefiting from the journalistic labour of professionals (McEnnis, 2017). Sports journalists are inadvertently preventing attempts by supporters' groups to gain closer access

Sports blogging 37

to the clubs that they feel alienated from and exercise their own version of accountability. Such discourses are clearly efforts at, to use Carlson's (2015) schematic, expulsion. Occasionally, sports journalists have achieved the ejection of those who are considered to be outside the occupational group. Football website Scotzine had its accreditation revoked by the Scottish Football Association (SFA) amid complaints from the mainstream media. The editor, Andy Muirhead, broke an embargo not to publish comments at a post-match press conference until the following day, which he stated was an "innocent mistake". Muirhead said that he received an e-mail from a journalist accusing his website of being a 'hobby' (Press Gazette, 2011). Here, Muirhead's failure to follow the sacred cow of obeying embargoes, an action that is seen as vital to the co-operative relationship between gatekeeper and journalists, proved costly. However, there are serious questions for sports journalists as to whether their access is as exclusive as they think. Lowes and Robillard (2018) state that:

> While sport journalists once traded on their access to the inside story around sport culture and their ability to bring it to their audience, audiences now have access to televised media conferences and official websites and can also follow the latest tweets and other social-media publications from key sport figures. Sometimes social-media users may also have access to behind-the-scenes information about players and teams (e.g., player injuries and trades). As a result of this shift, sport journalists no longer have a monopoly over ringside seats.
>
> (Lowes & Robillard, 2018, p. 310)

Eldridge (2018) notes how the journalistic discourse around disruptors is to effectively pillory them for style over substance and their "attention-grabbing sensationalism, contravening core tenets of the field" (p. 863). However, there are times when a blogger is recognised as authoritative, particularly if it is a story that can then be followed up by the mainstream media, labelled as "journalistic realisation". Certainly, it is difficult for professional sports journalists to ignore a story that originates in the blogosphere, particularly if it gains traction by going viral on social media. Eldridge (2018), in using Deadspin as a case study, concludes that journalistic discourse around bloggers has evolved to be less 'parasitical' in narrative, "where commentary and coverage originating on journalism's periphery can contribute to, rather than distract from, the work of the journalistic core" (p. 875). Sports journalists are also coming to the realisation that they are not the only ones with insider information. Sports lawyers and business experts have developed their own blogs that provide insights into professional sport that may be beyond the experience and knowledge of journalists (McEnnis, 2021b).

Sports journalists must carefully manage the narrative around the blogosphere's ability to break important news so that it is not presented as a professional failure on their part. Since 2016, the website Football Leaks has published documents that have demonstrated the murky goings-on in professional sport in terms of transfer dealings and financial accounting. The blogger, Rui Pinto, was quickly adopted by sports journalists at *Der Spiegel*, who helped to write a book on this matter (Buschmann & Wulzinger, 2018). Pinto therefore shifted from being a disruptor who was shining a light on journalistic failing to being a legitimate source who enabled sports reporters to demonstrate their ability to make good contacts and generate exclusivity. Further, *The Times* sportswriter Matthew Syed wrote a column that urged readers to see Football Leaks as being more about "an issue of transparency and secrecy at the top rather than a failure of sports journalism" (Syed, 2016). However, Pinto's later arrest for alleged computer hacking and subsequent charges of blackmail and extortion have since created uncomfortable ethical questions for sports journalists who both endorsed and legitimised Football Leaks (McEnnis, 2021b).

Similar ethical issues have been presented by the Russian cyberespionage group Fancy Bear, who hacked the World Anti-Doping Agency's database and leaked details of athletes' approved use of therapeutic-use exemptions (TUEs), which allow athletes to take otherwise banned substances for medical conditions (Ingle, 2016). Sports journalists have been more than happy to seize the narrative and take it into more legitimate newsgathering spaces, such as media briefings and press conferences (McEnnis, 2021b). However, the origins of the story in computer hacking were quickly forgotten and overshadowed by outrage towards the cycling team, Team Sky, and its main cyclists, such as Bradley Wiggins and Chris Froome. The manner in which sports journalists have readily accepted and adopted leaks from Football Leaks and Fancy Bear with scant reflection have done little to dispel the 'toy department' claims that they have a weak commitment to ethical conduct.

Blurring of boundaries: The sports journalist as blogger

The Guardian Sports Network, which is designed to provide a platform for amateur bloggers, also includes blogs from professional sports writers. For example, *The Guardian*'s chief football writer Jonathan

Liew wrote an article on legendary spin bowler Shane Warne's dream party that he had produced for The Nightwatchman, a collection of long-form writing about Australian cricket (Liew, 2020). Sports journalists' occupation of participatory spaces enables them to attempt to connect more with fans, while trading off the cultural cache of the blogosphere, and reach a youth demographic (Dart, 2009; Hutchins & Mikosza, 2010). The idea of journalists using blogs is not specific to sports journalism but also exists in the political sphere (Hermida, 2009). However, journalism's involvement in blogging is motivated by the desire to professionalise amateur spaces and formats (Singer, 2005; Thurman, 2008). Social media has contributed to a crisis of objectivity in journalism whereby the industry has expressed fears that journalists are becoming too subjective and biased. The new BBC director-general Tim Davie issued new social media guidance to his journalists in October 2020 for them not to "express a personal opinion on matters of public policy, politics, or controversial subjects" (BBC, 2020a).

Indeed, sports journalists are going further in their relationship with bloggers. Professional sports journalists are now inhabiting recognisably amateur spaces. It is no longer unusual to see a sports journalist as a guest or even a main presenter on a fan-produced podcast. A case study here is the Football Ramble, which takes an irreverent look at global football issues in the UK. In the 2017/18 season, the Football Ramble started producing the "On the Continent" show that included football journalists James Horncastle and Andy Brassell. *The Guardian* journalists Jonathan Wilson and Nicky Bandini have also contributed to the Football Ramble, while Kate Mason, of Sky Sports News, now presents shows (Baxter, 2020). These podcast appearances signpost journalists as the cultural authorities of sport, aligns them with fans rather than commercialised sports and imbues them with cultural cache. It is effectively the reverse of the Grantland-Bill Simmons case study that was analysed earlier in this chapter where the blogger entered the professional space. From the podcast's point of view, the sports journalist's appearance bestows an amateur space with legitimacy, credibility and even celebrity.

Sports journalism has been strongly influenced by the conventions, style, tone and language of blogging, despite decrying the blogosphere for its lack of professional standards (McEnnis, 2017). Bloggers adopt a more personal and informal tone that helps them to connect with audiences (Carlson, 2017; Serazio, 2021). Sports journalists have attempted similar approaches in their digital strategies. Live blogging is a journalistic format that thrives on its informality, and the shared virtual experience of digital journalists watching a sports event on television alongside their audience helps them to connect and build community (McEnnis, 2016). Journalism in general has undergone a shift in recent history from rejecting blogging to accepting it as a practice (Carlson & Lewis, 2015). However, this engagement with blogging is in danger of taking sports journalists further down the route of opinion, subjectivity and analysis – rather than hard news – as they become more like armchair bloggers despite their access to professional sport (Daum & Scherer, 2018).

Conclusion

Sports journalists have found it impossible to prevent bloggers from using their norms, forms and styles in the digital age. Instead, their focus has shifted towards patrolling their boundaries and attempting to determine which bloggers are allowed to enter the professional field. Certainly, sports journalists have favoured bloggers who do not conflict with their core beat routines and offer opportunities to expand content on digital platforms (McEnnis, 2017). It could be argued that sports journalists have been less interested in collaborating with audiences in the production of more serious journalism, even though scholars recognise that there are opportunities to be had (Forde & Wilson 2018; Rowe, 2017). Regardless of professional approval, alternative sites, such as Deadspin, have helped to expand the different possibilities in which sports journalism can be approached. Sports journalism has seen its boundaries expand as it has become a practice conducted by both professionals and amateurs. This development has contributed to a broader news agenda and helped to bring minority voices and marginalised issues to the forefront of public discourse.

Sports journalists have responded by increasing their visibility across professional and amateur spaces. The power of the mainstream media in terms of resources and audiences also provides sports journalists with leverage over bloggers. Nevertheless, sports journalists have been confronted with the need to justify their professional position with so many other voices now entering the communication process. Sports journalists have clung on to their access to professional sport as a vital boundary marker between themselves and bloggers. However, this approach is becoming increasingly limited as bloggers and influencers start to insert themselves into the press pack. Sports journalists are attempting to discursively protect their privileged position. However, accreditation is ultimately the decision of media managers, who may increasingly determine attendees on their audience reach and public profile. If so, such a policy may not be to the benefit of sports journalists. Sports journalists should, then, be less fixated about their access to professional sport and think more deeply about how they can use their skills and experience to work with bloggers on issues of public and societal significance.

4 Sports public relations

Sports journalism is heavily reliant on the public relations industry for its source environment. An essential part of sports journalists' work routines is to access professional athletes and coaches. As interest in sports has grown and media exposure increased, so has the need to develop narratives surrounding the sports event in a 24-hour news culture (Sugden & Tomlinson, 2010). Journalists have a crucial role to play in keeping audiences engaged with sports even when nothing is happening on the field of play. While 24-hour news channels started to fill that void in the late 1990s, this constant diet of reporting the words that come out of the mouths of sports celebrities has accelerated further with the omnipresence of digital and social media.

One of the stronger criticisms of sports journalism is that journalists operate in a narrow source environment that has led to a cosy relationship with professional sport (Sugden & Tomlinson, 2007). Sports journalists are considered to have sacrificed their core principles of independence and autonomy to maintain their access. However, as professional sport has become increasingly commercialised, digitised and globalised, journalists have found it more difficult to gain access to these sources. At a time when journalists are feeling a stronger need than ever to access players and athletes to service an always-on news culture, "in a self perpetuating cycle ... even if there is nothing necessarily newsworthy to report" (Sherwood, Nicholson & Marjoribanks, 2017a, p. 1005), they are finding it more challenging to access them.

Sports journalists experienced good access to coaches and athletes in the past because the balance of power was in their favour. Communication technology and infrastructure were scarce and expensive and the sole domain of media organisations (Hutchins & Rowe, 2009). Sports clubs and organisations recognised the only way they could gain publicity for their activities was via sports journalists. Similarly, public relations departments realised that they could gain vast amounts of

DOI: 10.4324/9781003106869-4

publicity if they provided "regular, high-quality information subsidies that facilitate newswork" (Sherwood, Nicholson & Marjoribanks, 2017a, p. 1005). However, television and radio have expanded through globalisation (Lowes & Robillard, 2018). Broadcasters pay significant sums of money in exchange for the right to show professional sport and, in addition, are exacting access demands to players and coaches for interviews. The press has found itself increasingly marginalised as the financial clout of broadcast has become the primary media force in professional sport, to the point where it effectively bankrolls the industry. The press is low down the list of sports clubs' access priorities because of their lack of economic muscle. Print sports journalists simply cannot compete with this financial weight being thrown around by the broadcast industry.

Clubs and organisations have also developed their own media platforms, such as websites, web TV and social media channels, so they can now bypass journalists and communicate directly to their fans and audiences (Sherwood, Nicholson & Marjoribanks, 2017b; Suggs, 2016). Digital technology has emerged alongside, and in connection with, a development in promotional culture that has become more brand and image conscious. The power balance has shifted away from sports journalists and towards the sources, clubs and organisations themselves.

Public relations departments have expanded exponentially in terms of resources and personnel to produce their own media platforms. Here, a distinction needs to be made between two typologies of public relations that are impacting on sports journalism. The first is the classic public relations role that involves administering access to what are described as 'information subsidies', which are "pre-packaged information for use by media that aims to reduce the cost of producing news" (Sherwood, Nicholson & Marjoribanks, 2017a, p. 994). In the case of sports, these information subsidies take the form of press conferences and media briefings that sports journalists must attend on-site at training grounds or sports stadia and which involve securing accreditation from media managers who work for these news organisations. The second is content production roles where public relations personnel must produce stories, videos and audios for the media platforms. These two typologies of public relations have a symbiotic relationship – the need to provide content for media platforms has a direct influence on how media managers grant access and to who.

Sports journalists have a shared occupational culture globally in the way that press conferences and media briefings are primary sources of news. However, different territories have slightly different experiences in their interactions with professional sport. For example, journalistic access in the US is regarded as better than in the UK because there is a will to protect it in the codes and constitutions of the leagues themselves (Curtis, 2019). However, sports journalists in the US are becoming increasingly concerned that shifts in the sport–media complex prompted by digital technology are leading to greater constraints. The fact that the literature referenced in this chapter draws from the US, UK and Australian contexts demonstrates this is a shared concern across sports journalism's community of practice.

Inside out: The changing boundaries of access

Journalistic access to professional sport has become increasingly controlled and monitored by public relations personnel as media managers have inserted themselves as a layer between reporters and athletes and coaches (Sherwood, Nicholson & Marjoribanks, 2017a; Suggs, 2016). Sports journalists are reliant on media managers in setting the codes and rules of engagement. Suggs (2016) points out in his case study of US college sports, "reporters ... have no guaranteed privileges in the press box or the locker room" (p. 275). It is instead the public relations departments that control the news flows and agendas (Sherwood, Nicholson & Marjoribanks, 2017a). In tightly restricting the sites of news generation, media managers are having a major influence on journalistic practice.

Daum and Scherer (2018) argue that "sports journalists are increasingly vulnerable to coercion and the expectation that they will fulfil the promotional wishes of major league sport in exchange for continued access, albeit in a radically reduced form" (p. 565). There is a self-awareness of this approach within professional sport as well, with football manager Nigel Pearson describing it as "moving towards a dictatorial state" (Sharman, 2021). Sports journalists' increasing reliance on a narrow source environment of professional sport vastly reduces their autonomy in the generation of news. Sports clubs and organisations, as gatekeepers, recognise the power they have over journalists. Reflecting their status as 'official' sources, media managers' version of events and reality is definitive even though their agenda, to protect the brand, makes them potentially unreliable and leaves the possibility for untruths (Lowes, 1999; Sherwood, Nicholson & Marjoribanks, 2017a). Further, the beat system is about highly routinised and rhythmic content production rather than visiting stories on newsworthiness alone (Sherwood, Nicholson & Marjoribanks, 2017a).

Also, public relations in sport is more about limiting and denying, rather than facilitating, access to sources. Athletes and coaches are media trained to say as little as possible in the presence of journalists (Rowe, 2015). Media managers' decisions on who to admit to press conferences has also become skewed. 'Good' sports journalism is subverted in these settings to mean passivity and complicity, while asking important and searching questions is construed as being difficult or troublemaking. Sports journalists who do not conform have their accreditation revoked. Further, closely controlled press conferences also create intimidating, confrontational and adversarial atmospheres that, when combined with sexist attitudes from within professional sport, are particularly hostile environments for women sports journalists. In 2017, *Charlotte Observer* sports journalist Jourdan Rodrigue's question to Carolina Panthers quarterback Cam Newton at a press conference was met with derision as the NFL player stated: "It's funny to hear a female talk about routes" (McKenzie & Fisher, 2017).

Media managers' instrumental control over sports journalists is further enabled by the international composition of the press pack. Sports journalists' ability to operate effectively within staged events, such as press conferences or media briefings, is diluted by the global circus that exists in major leagues. Here, demand to attend press conferences and media briefings can outstrip supply, leading to even greater pressure on sports journalists to curry favour with media managers. Global media operate with diverse and sometimes conflicting agendas that are often drawn along national lines. For example, a South Korean journalist at a Tottenham Hotspur press conference is likely to focus on the forward Son Heung-Min, regardless of the player's recent accomplishments. However, a sports journalist working for the English media will take a more holistic view, knowing that the team in general is of interest to their audience. Such a fragmented approach to interviewing makes it easier for sports organisations and clubs to escape scrutiny as the press pack is unable to act as a coherent questioning unit that represents shared agendas. Sports journalists as a collective are unable to mobilise and co-ordinate themselves effectively. Also, the global nature of media means that public relations managers must first satisfy the multiple television rights holders before they can turn their attention to the print media.

A further ethical challenge for journalists that exists beyond press conferences and briefings is the day-to-day deals that they broker with the professional sport environment, particularly in terms of how they access players. Often sports journalists need to negotiate with the athlete's sponsors, marketeers and management companies to gain access.

These talks often result in the surrendering of editorial control. The lack of power that sports journalists possess in such a relationship means that they agree to copy approval and other promotional coverage to ensure they acquire the big interview (McEnnis, 2018a). Sports journalists' reliance on narrow sources and their lack of power within the sports–media complex means misplaced loyalties and lack of transparency can ensue. Reed and Harrison's (2019) study of unnamed sources in sports journalism finds that the majority of National Basketball Association (NBA) trades were unsourced, although there was no greater success of predictions in stories that included named sources. Reed and Harrison (2019) discover that sports journalism all too easily anonymises its sources and finds itself at the centre of a political struggle between players, agents and clubs. Here, sports journalists can be exploited in attempting to engineer moves from players. The existence of trade and transfer deadlines in professional sport creates particularly intensive periods of gossip, rumour and speculation.

The changing nature of the source environment has reshaped the boundaries of sports journalists' practices in how they build and cultivate contacts and with whom. The ability to build relationships and develop contacts with key sport personnel is pivotal to the occupational culture of sports journalism. McEnnis (2018a) notes that, in the past, sports journalists could be hired for their contacts book, with their social skills taking precedence over other expected journalistic qualities, such as writing ability and ethical conduct. However, Boyle (2013) argues that sports journalists discursively embellish how close they are to a source, which he describes as the "myth of access" (p. 95). Sports journalists continue to present a narrative of close source relations even though this is increasingly looking to be harder to achieve. Sports journalists must maximise the paucity of access that they do receive and ensure they generate as much copy out of it as possible. There are various journalistic devices that are also employed to give this impression, such as the posed photograph of journalist with athlete. Hidden from view is the watchful eye of media managers who are very quick to prevent questioning on topics that do not comply with strategic goals, and, invariably, these off-limits subjects are the most newsworthy and important ones.

The third-party arrangements that sports clubs are likely to be interested in approving in future include fly-on-the-wall access to streaming services such as Amazon Prime and Netflix. In the UK in recent years, Manchester City, Tottenham Hotspur and Juventus have struck deals with Netflix to give them insider access and produce a docu-drama behind the scenes of the club, called All or Nothing. Such commercial partnerships also mean that sports journalists are even lower on the list of priorities when it comes to access. However, this programming is heavily promotional and substantially edited to present favourable impressions of the club that have been described as a "glossy club commercial" (Hattenstone, 2018). It also raises questions over who has editorial control – the club or the programme makers. Further, the docu-drama represents a parody of investigative journalism in which no questions are asked about the fact that Manchester City are owned by the royal family of a country, United Arab Emirates, with human-rights issues (Hattenstone, 2018).

However, Boyle (2021) offers the view that "they provide some form of long-form journalism at a time when the written equivalent … appears to become more and more niche" and that they are becoming an "increasingly important part of the wider journalistic landscape that engages, mediates and makes sense of the complex world of sport" (p. 357). Certainly, the pursuit of ratings may lead to potentially revealing situations, such as when the Tottenham player Danny Rose had an argument with manager Jose Mourinho and stormed out of the office (Varley, 2020). After all, such behind-the-scenes events are usually concealed from journalists. Ultimately, what docu-dramas do or do not show are the outcomes of negotiations with the clubs themselves where commercial arguments foreground public-interest claims. As a consequence, docu-dramas will continue to be inconsistent in what they reveal and these editorial choices will be driven by entertainment and commercial values rather than journalistic ones.

From sources to rivals: The rise of team media

Sports leagues and clubs, in their quest for global economic growth, have developed their own form of what is known as 'team media' in the way that they have "institutionalized a range of digital production strategies and employ an increasing number of personnel to write stories, capture audio and video and engage with fans via social media" (Daum & Scherer, 2018, p. 562). This development has disrupted the journalist–source power dynamic further in that sports clubs and organisations see the mainstream media as clashing with their own strategic goals. In short, the sources have become competitors, which is problematic for the mainstream media. Lowes and Robillard (2018) describe this as a process whereby "sport reporters are becoming social-media content creators and curators while competing against spectator sport-content creators" (p. 309). In the immediate aftermath of Premier League football matches in the UK, journalists are herded into confined physical spaces, known as mixed zones, with media managers carefully selecting the athletes that will be presented to them for interviews. This system allows for media managers to potentially hold back the newsworthy, sought-after athletes for the club's own digital communication channels. Sherwood, Nicholson and Marjoribanks (2017b) found that media managers see traditional media as the domain for breaking news. However, club media are increasingly using the norms of sports journalism in the way that they tag 'exclusives' on their own news. Media managers employ protectionist tactics with the imposition of embargos on sports journalists, which delay their ability to run stories. These embargos are often motivated by the fact that clubs wish to break news on their own channels first. It is actually this very exclusion of mainstream media that allows the clubs and organisations to drive larger audiences to their content.

Sherwood, Nicholson and Marjoribanks (2017a), in their interviews with Australian sports journalists, found that one participant had their fifth athlete request approved because the other requests did not fit with the club's strategic goals. Meanwhile, team media personnel do not need to seek media managers' permission in the same way that sports journalists do – they are direct work colleagues, after all – and can access players and coaches directly (Sherwood, Nicholson & Marjoribanks, 2017b). The fact that professional sport is now effectively in competition with the mainstream media has created additional tension, instability and uncertainty for sports journalism that was already being fuelled by its struggles for access to professional sport in general (Lowes & Robillard, 2018).

Clubs and leagues, in growing their team media departments, have emerged as major employers of sports journalists. Team media are now providing a fruitful and stable employment option for both laid-off sports journalists and graduates entering the field. Hutchins and Boyle (2017) note that "career opportunities in communications and public relations are 'booming' compared to journalism" (p. 505). Here, clubs utilise the newsgathering, writing, multimedia and interviewing skills of both trained and experienced sports journalists to produce content for their digital and social media platforms. The move from journalism into public relations has always existed, which led to the phrase 'poachers turned gamekeepers' in reference to the shifting role from information gatherers to gatekeepers (Nicholls, 2019). Sports journalism is criticised for being 'cheerleaders' to the clubs and leagues it covers (Boyle, 2006; Lowes, 1999; Rowe, 2004) so the transition to public relations is seen as an easy one to make. Further, team media are similar to sports journalism in character, norms and values, which has led Mirer (2019) to argue that the move to public relations is no longer the paradigmatic, epistemological and professional shift it once was.

However, a key point of departure between sports journalism and public relations is motivation. Daum and Scherer (2018) observe that team media do not "follow a journalistic code of ethics, but rather a code of corporate/promotional conduct, which seeks to protect a brand and market share" (p. 563). Certainly, journalists' professional claims of autonomy, independence, objectivity and public service are highly attractive to sports organisations looking to gain legitimacy and credibility on their digital platforms. In employing journalists, these sport organisations can obfuscate the cynicism of their corporate motives. Mirer's (2019) interviews with US sports journalists who moved from legacy, traditional media to team media reveal they consider themselves as retaining their membership of the occupational community despite now effectively working in public relations. These journalists-turned-team media writers do not consider themselves as compromising on their beliefs and values despite working within a different corporate logic. Also, sports journalists as content creators position themselves in a separate space to the media manager/gatekeepers discussed in the previous section of this chapter. Mirer (2019) argues that "... leaving the newsroom for public relations is a time-honored tradition in journalism. Yet in-house sports reporters reject the idea that moving to these outlets mean that they have done that" (p. 81).

The recruitment of high-profile sports journalists from legacy news media suggests not only that team media are the main place to consume sports content but that they constitute a new, reworked journalism. Team media personnel roles are described as 'in-club' journalists, which, far from semantics, is ideologically important in how these employers see what they are doing. This recruitment strategy also offers a fascinating contrast to the news industry's shift away from job titles that include 'journalist' and towards content producers, as discussed in Chapter 2. At a time when the news industry is looking to move away from journalistic legitimacy, the public relations sector is actively moving towards and embracing it. However, public relations' notion of what its journalists are is very different to legacy understandings. As Mirer (2019) notes, team media use a discourse of objectivity as a way of legitimising their own work. The connection between journalists and their professional principles helps to mask the bias and myopia of team media platforms. Not only does the hiring of press sports journalists give greater authority and legitimacy to team media but it also allows them to enter the boundary contest of what sports journalism should be. Such discourses generally exclude criticality, scrutiny and public interest and prioritise soft, promotional, multimedia content and consumer engagement. Mirer's interviews with 24 team media employees found that they value accuracy yet shy away from negative stories about their employers. Mirer (2019) states:

> Facts are often bad for a given team, in-house sports reporters must address defeats and slumps on a regular basis. Their response is to focus on data and quotations; using numbers to establish performance issues and yielding to the expertise of coaches and players for analysis ... team websites are less likely to engage in reporter-driven analysis.
>
> (Mirer, 2019, p. 77)

In Mirer's study, in-house reporters see themselves as accountable to the public rather than the sports organisations they work for, in keeping with their journalistic heritage. Yet their approach to news work is clearly with their employer's strategic goals firmly in mind. Mirer (2019) also states, "in-house reporters do not spend much time talking about why their work matters beyond its commercial function for the team" (p. 83). Here, team media are not places where we can expect to see exposés on FIFA corruption and the concussion crisis in American football. Team media also re-define quality as being 'official' and present the fact that the news is generated by the source itself as meaning it is authentic (Mirer, 2019). Further blurring the boundaries is the finding that news organisations would be prepared to employ people from team media backgrounds as journalists, prompting Mirer (2019) to argue that "if journalism treats in-house positions as just another reporting job ... in-house reporters are arguing themselves into the profession" (p. 82).

This blurring of boundaries between sports journalism and team media is also causing confusion for the sports industry, particularly in the conferring of awards. Mirer (2019) notes that in-house journalists have inserted themselves into key award ceremonies, such as the Baseball Writers' Association of America, which also provides them with legitimacy and authority. However, this is not a consistent picture as the Sports Journalists' Association (SJA) in the UK does not recognise team media in its annual awards (Sports Journalists' Association, 2021). Further, the presence of team media members on voting panels for sports awards has caused consternation because of concerns over bias and partisanship. Sports broadcasters employed by teams for their own channels were banned from voting in the end-of-season awards for the National Basketball Association (NBA) in 2017 (Birdsong, 2017). Here, the votes are important in determining players' salaries and the presence of team media was perceived as a conflict of interest. Clearly, then, professional sport does see a need for independent media in certain situations. However, the NBA decision assumes that the independent media is truly independent rather than being cheerleaders for the teams they cover (Boyle, 2006; Rowe, 2004). Nevertheless, such boundaries being drawn provide vital room for sports journalists to propound a discourse of independence and autonomy and highlight the conflicts and ethical failings of team media.

Content production has also become broader than team channels to include individual athlete accounts. Team media or social agencies can either post directly on behalf of athletes or generate the material for the account holder to activate. This raises the issue of transparency and authenticity to fans. Sunderland footballer Victor Anichebe rather inadvertently laid the process bare following a 1–0 defeat by West Ham by tweeting, "Can you tweet something like Unbelievable support yesterday and great effort by the lads! Hard result to take! But we go again" (De Menezes, 2016). A case of mistaken identity took place after two players on the same social media agency's books were confused with each other. Manchester City's John Stones Instagram account posted, "Great win today and congratulations @alvaromorata on his hat-trick! #CFC", which was actually meant for Chelsea defender Gary Cahill and related to a game that Stones was not involved in (McMullan, 2017). There is little that is ethical about making audiences believe that the words originated from someone else and it raises issues for direct communication from athletes to fans without the mediation of sports journalists. A lack of moral compass also manifests itself in other ways on team media. In 2020, the Leeds United official Twitter account, which had 664,000 followers at the time, mocked Amazon Prime Sport pundit Karen Carney for questioning the club's staying power due to their high-tempo playing style. The tweet, which used laughter emojis next to pull quotes of what Carney said, led to more than 4,000 responses, many of which were sexist and abusive (Ingle, 2020). As a result, Carney, a former England footballer, deleted her own Twitter account. Team media clearly wield considerable power on social media in the way that they can mobilise their user fanbase, and potentially weaponise it. However, whether they exercise the same level of ethical responsibility as we would expect from journalists and independent news organisations is questionable.

Pushing back: Sports journalism's acts of resistance

Given such an overwhelming power imbalance, why are journalists still given access to professional sport at all? For now, media managers still recognise there is inherent value in hosting sports journalists, although there is a lack of a coherent strategy. Sherwood, Nicholson and Marjoribanks (2017b) note that media managers make decisions on "where stories should be placed – i.e. traditional media or on their own platforms – ... on a case by case basis" (p. 519). Media managers recognise their own platforms are generally restricted to their fan base whereas the mainstream media have access to wider audiences. This approach is usually informed by the desire of sponsors to gain as much exposure as possible (Sherwood, Nicholson & Marjoribanks, 2017b). Further, sports journalists are seen to imbue promotional information with a credibility and authority that ensures its successful messaging, transmission and influence on receivers. Public relations departments are beginning to think their work relationship with athletes and coaches, as essentially wider colleagues, can inform their own storytelling more strongly than independent media. The irony is that it is media managers' own actions in controlling access that have led to a distance and impersonality between sports journalists and athletes and coaches. Also, in keeping the production of news in-house, public relations departments have greater control over how a story is presented and packaged.

There are, however, interesting signs of resistance from sports journalists, who are expressing their professional frustrations at tightly controlled access on digital and social media. Sports journalists can use these restrictions and censorship to assert that their attempts at 'good' journalism are being thwarted. Here, sports journalists can remind the public of the clear distinctions between themselves and team media. Sports journalists being denied access has also enabled them to signal their professional credibility. News organisations can argue that upsetting clubs is a sign that sports journalists are not towing the corporate line and that they are acting as independent, truth-seeking journalists with a willingness to ask the difficult questions. This development is impossible to separate from digital technology. Social media enable sports journalists to express a discourse of professionalism that can be reputation enhancing. However, the notion of sports journalists acting in the public interest is a complex one and does not always curry favour among the tribalism of sports fans. For example, one journalist revealed that he cancelled an interview as he was unable to ask a question on Black Lives Matter to England football captain Harry Kane (Pellatt, 2020). The fact that an article is written on a non-interview demonstrates an interesting discursive technique whereby journalists can claim to be frustrated in their public-service commitments by being censored within professional sport.

Associated Press journalist Rob Harris was met with backlash from Manchester City manager Pep Guardiola for asking a searching question about a potential breach of financial fair play rules (FFP) in the press conference following the club winning the FA Cup in 2019, thus securing a domestic treble. Guardiola stated: "Do you know the question you're asking me, if I ever received money for another situation, right now, today?" Harris also found himself criticised by other media workers, with television pundit and former footballer Danny Murphy describing it as "attention seeking" and "ego driven" (O'Brien, 2019). However, Harris defended himself by pointing to the value of truth-seeking journalism in both his Twitter posts and wider media appearances. Harris tweeted:

> The media's job isn't to be cheerleaders. Easier life not to ask challenging questions of clubs we have dealings with and know. But that would be doing a disservice. Acclaiming performances of players can be separated from the need to report the surrounding circumstances at clubs.

In an appearance on the podcast Off The Ball AM, Harris further elaborated on the decision behind his actions by stating that the question had first been posed to the club six months previously and had not been met with an answer, which resulted in Guardiola himself being put in a difficult position (O'Donnell, 2019). It is difficult not to see Harris' own reaction as important boundary work in reasserting the importance of independent journalism in highly constrained circumstances, although the criticism from within the media also demonstrates the internal pressure on journalists not to break from the promotional function by being inquisitive and critical of professional sport. However, while this plays out well on social media for sports journalism, it should, ultimately, not detract from the conflict between coach and reporters, which rarely yields answers to questions.

Trinity Mirror's digital publishing director David Higgerson argues on his personal blog that sports journalists having their access and accreditation withdrawn could be a positive development. He said:

> There are times when a ban can perhaps even be a blessing. While it's remarkable that Blackpool FC ... feels it can afford to cut off relations with the local Blackpool Gazette, surely it gives the Gazette the chance to demonstrate its independence from the club ... and it's that objectivity which will resonate with fans longer than any ban.
>
> (Higgerson, 2015)

In 2012, Bournemouth FC withdrew the accreditation of the local paper, the *Bournemouth Echo*, for what it perceived as negative coverage. The *Bournemouth Echo* responded by carrying a front-page editorial headlined "Banned" (*Bournemouth Echo*, 2012). In this article, the *Bournemouth Echo*, clearly not cowed by the ban, drew attention to the fact that the club had received more than 700 back pages since the then-chairman had taken charge in 2009, promotional coverage that was the equivalent of £840,000 in advertising revenue. "So our message ... is this, give our advertising representatives a call, because the days of editorial backing for your football club are over until such time as you come to terms with what 'free press' means" (*Bournemouth Echo*, 2012). Here, the *Bournemouth Echo* is pointing to both the promotional and journalistic value of what it does – a dual discourse that is aimed at both the club and its readers.

Sports journalists have also been prepared to demonstrate creativity and imagination in attempting to overcome the limitations that are imposed on the media at press briefings. One Spanish reporter showed initiative when the press was told Atletico Madrid footballer Antoine Griezmann would only be answering questions in French because of rumours that he was joining another club. This was a clear example of a public relations strategy that was exploiting the global composition of press conferences. Pedro Morata, of radio station Cadena SER, decided to overcome this limitation by using Google Translate to turn his question from Spanish to French. Press officer Philippe Tornon told Griezmann not to answer the question even though the footballer himself could see the funny side (Richards, 2018). Such boldness and innovation demonstrated in the case studies above are a counter-reaction to the coercion and intimidation by public relations departments. Sports journalists need to continue to resist and disrupt the tightly controlled conditions that have been created. Bans from press conferences are stories in themselves and sports journalists can enhance their authority by pointing to the narrative that independent journalism is being suppressed and denied. Further, media managers can look heavy-handed and unfair, thus negating the effectiveness of their public relations strategies.

Conclusion

Within the sociology of professions, public relations is considered to be the biggest single threat to journalists' boundaries. Abbott (1988, p. 225) notes that "mobility between journalism and public relations is quite common". However, Abbott also points out that journalists were

Sports public relations 55

keen to establish separate and distinct rules from publicity professionals. Abbott uses the example of *The New York Times* journalists in the 1920s being alarmed at the involvement of publicity agents in providing half of stories, which was seen by journalists as essentially advertising and an affront to their normative principles. This led to a greater push for founding professional structures and to update the professional code.

Changes in the balance of power in the sport–media complex have led to public relations strategies effectively reshaping the boundaries of journalistic practice. Sports journalists are now building contacts and relationships with media managers rather than the athletes and coaches they cover. Journalists are also restricted from asking certain questions in press briefings and they are threatened with bans should they demonstrate critical inquiry. Media managers have also reduced journalists' autonomy and independence due to their tight control over access to professional sport. Sports journalists are pressured to produce complicit and favourable coverage to ensure their continued accreditation.

Public relations is also reshaping who is considered to be a sports journalist and what sports journalism is. Sports clubs, leagues and organisations now employ "in-club journalists" to provide content to their digital platforms. These roles are often filled by sports journalists who have either been laid off by news organisations or are tempted by better pay and conditions. This recruitment strategy is blurring the boundaries of both who constitutes a sports journalist and what constitutes sports journalism. In the hands of in-club journalists, discourses on practice are likely to be motivated by brand image rather than public service. This chapter has also demonstrated the lack of ethical principles underpinning team media content. The future employment trend is also likely to see team media personnel continuing to expand, with the news industry contracting its workforce.

Sports journalism has shown a rather inconsistent approach to protecting its boundaries from the public relations industry. As Mirer (2019) has noted, news organisations are content to 'reverse' recruiting in-club journalists. However, sports journalists have developed counter-narratives to their bans from professional sport or their restricted access that enable them to reinforce their professional principles. Sports journalists can take to their social media accounts and wider media to highlight their martyrdom in attempting to hold power to account. Such rhetoric is important boundary work from sports journalists and should embolden them in taking greater stands to the public relations industry. The journalism industry also needs to consider important questions about whether it is doing enough to challenge and critique in-club journalism and strongly consider whether they should accept team media as "one of their own". By passively integrating team media into the community of practice, the journalism industry is not doing enough to consider the different sets of motivations that underpin both team media and sports journalism.

The prognosis for sports journalists' accreditation to professional sport is not good. Their access is likely to be restricted further as the digital platforms of clubs, leagues and organisations continue to evolve. Team media strategies are also likely to be more akin to news organisations in the way that they will see access and appeal to wider audiences as essential to growing the fan/customer base. Team media will continue to look to reshape the journalistic discourse by situating storytelling within strategic goals. Certainly, Premier League football clubs are looking to expand their media operations and invest significant sums of revenue as they recognise their importance in growing the global brand. Also, professional sport organisations are recognising that media products give them access to data on the audiences that they attract. As Joseph (2020) notes, football clubs are "changing from a typical sponsorship model towards one more focused on content creation and distribution".

The solution to the problems presented in this chapter is for journalists to realise that adopting critical and questioning approaches to professional sport is vital in distinguishing them from team media. Sports journalists have a reputation as cheerleaders for the teams they cover, but they are now confronted by team media, whose overt purpose is to be cheerleaders. Sports journalists need to re-inforce their ethical conduct and emphasise how much more valuable and important their professional principles are for society. Sports journalists must remember that their loyalties are with the public and not the sources they cover. Sports journalists need to push back on automatically granting sources, such as player agents, anonymity, and be more transparent in their journalism to restore public trust.

5 Athlete sports journalism

Historically, tensions within sports journalism have had a technological dimension. The emergence of radio and television forced sports journalism to evolve its principles and practices to survive. The immediacy that these platforms provided displaced sports journalists' purpose to relay the live event to sports fans who could not be present at the stadium. Sports journalists responded by evolving to "offer analysis and opinion to sporting matters, rather than simply reporting sporting events" (Boyle, 2006, p. 76) while also exploring "scene-setting, pre and post-event analysis and, in some cases, scandal" (Daum & Scherer, 2018, p. 553). Print sports journalists' ability to survive both the advent of television and radio demonstrated an impressive adaptability and resilience (Boyle, 2006), although their core routines of building contacts, travelling to sports events and hitting deadlines went relatively unchanged (Daum & Scherer, 2018).

The advent of broadcast journalism also meant a new entrant to an ongoing boundary dispute over who lays claim to the definitive view of sports journalism. The debate within the print media of what constitutes 'good' sports journalism has been defined by differences between popular tabloid newspapers and the so-called quality broadsheets. Here, the broadsheet press emphasises good writing and contextual analysis, while the popular tabloids value speed and breaking news (Rowe, 2004). Definitions of good and desirable practice are also heavily informed by sport's links with class. For instance, there are often literary claims made by cricket writers that are reinforced by prestigious almanacs such as *Wisden* that speak to the upper-class connotations of the sport, whereas football writing is perceived to be more prosaic and functional in serving the working-class masses (Boyle & Haynes, 2009). The emergent tensions between print and broadcast sports journalists in the mid to late 20th century (Boyle, 2006) speak to a broader rivalry between these industries to be the cultural authorities and principal storytellers in journalism (Meltzer, 2009; Zelizer, 1992).

DOI: 10.4324/9781003106869-5

In the 1990s, newspaper sports journalists expressed fresh concerns over the advent of 24-hour rolling sports news and how this was leading to trivial and shallow content. In the digital age, television has increasingly moved away from professional journalists towards former athletes to tell its stories, and this trend is having an impact on the traditional press. This chapter considers how we arrived at this point in the internal competition within sports journalism concerning what constitutes expertise. It also analyses whether the increasing trend towards what will be termed 'athlete sports journalism' is having a beneficial or detrimental effect on professional quality.

Print versus broadcast sports journalism

There has been a long-standing tension between print and broadcast sports journalists in common with the wider industry, as chronicled in Zelizer's (1992) study of the John F Kennedy assassination. Whether broadcasting constitutes journalism has become contested as the press dismissed it as entertainment while broadcasters wanted to avoid a label that had rather negative connotations (Boyle, 2006). However, the emergence of 24-hour rolling sports news has changed the dynamic on that front. A recognisable television sports journalism has emerged that is very much emulative of the press and has caused further tension as it has moved beyond describing the sports event into the areas of breaking news, analysis and even, at times, scandal.

These tensions have heightened as print and broadcast journalists have sought to inhabit similar physical media spaces in the professional sport environment. Print sports journalists believe that the broadcast sports journalists get preferential treatment. However, journalistic access can be low on the list of priorities when live sports rights contracts are drawn up between broadcasters and professional leagues. Broadcast sports journalists, on the other hand, are envious that, away from the glare of the cameras, print sports journalists are perceived to have more intimate and revealing comments from sources. The feeling among broadcasters is that the guard is dropped with the press and they benefit from more open and honest dialogue, and therefore more newsworthy conversations and information. In contrast, broadcasters believe they get the carefully stage managed 'for television' interviews.

Digital technology has led to a further exacerbation of internal tensions and conflicts. The fact that all journalists can now publish immediately has disrupted the traditional boundaries between print and broadcast journalists, which were essentially marked along temporal lines. These new tensions can be seen in the shifts that have taken place in how

Premier League football press conferences are organised and staged. Print sports journalists had been given their own separate briefing because they were concerned their broadcast counterparts were able to immediately disseminate the news to the public and there was therefore nothing new to publish. However, additional measures needed to be put into place to ensure that the boundaries between broadcast and print could be maintained because now the newspaper reporters also had the power of immediacy through their social media channels. The response has been to use embargos, where a time delay is placed on the publication of information, to ensure sports journalists who work for news organisations that do not have the benefits of immediacy, such as daily and weekly newspapers, are able to write stories that are 'new'. Curtis (2019) outlines the way that press conferences in the UK are organised as follows:

> After a Saturday soccer match, a club's manager gives a press conference in front of the TV cameras … What the manager says can be used immediately, on TV or on Twitter. Then, the manager may hold a separate meeting with newspaper writers and answer more questions. What the manager says in *that* interview is embargoed, by agreement of the writers, until 10:30p.m. that night. No tweets, no early posts allowed … At a soccer manager's prematch press conference for a Sunday game, the daily newspaper writers get an embargoed press conference in the manner described above. Then the writers for Sunday papers like *The Sunday Times* and *The Mail on Sunday* get another press conference.
>
> (Curtis, 2019)

Curtis (2019) considers embargos to be "akin to World War II rationing". Sports journalists engage in a form of expulsion if its members fail to adhere to this system. Curtis (2019) describes an incident whereby Italian journalist Gianluca di Marzio broke an embargo and he was labelled among the press pack as a 'disgrace to the profession'. Embargos are an important means of ensuring boundaries between sports journalists working for different types of media in the UK. Curtis (2019) ponders whether it will eventually represent the future of US sports journalism as media access is likely to tighten further with the growth of the content economy of professional sport.

Salwen and Garrison's (1998) interviews with US press sports journalists find they considered their broadcast counterparts to have damaged the professional reputation because they "engage in cheerleader-type journalism for the home team" (p. 94). One sports journalist expressed vexation that broadcasters were impacting on his ability to perform his duties and recounted a tale when a locker-room interview with an American football player in the National Football League (NFL) was interrupted because the television network CBS was ready to talk to him. Sugden and Tomlinson (2010) expressed concerns that the UK 24-hour rolling news station Sky Sports News "escalates the profile of sports chatter and sports gossip to the centre of the communicative process" and, in doing so, has "threatened the wider journalistic principles that were established in the print media over the previous two centuries" (p. 164). Sugden and Tomlinson's (2010) interviewee, veteran sports journalist Mike Collett, argues that Sky Sports News was re-defining the news agenda towards hype and trivia that print journalists were obliged to follow. Collett also opined that print journalists were behind television and radio in the pecking order for player interviews and this meant "they have said the same thing half a dozen times already. By the time they get to you, unless they know you personally, they won't want to talk to you and they're off" (p. 162).

Sports broadcasters started to recognise the importance of building greater prestige and status into their brand and provide a counter-reaction to 24-hour rolling news, while also expanding into new markets and arenas of competition. This led to an increased interest in documentary programming. Similar to Sky Sports News, the US sports broadcasting giant ESPN faced accusations that it "lacks journalistic integrity, privileges sensationalized speculation and hype to covering actual sporting events and spends far too much time focusing on – and amplifying – the scandals surrounding the sports world" (Vogan, 2012, p. 138). In 2008, ESPN created a film production arm called ESPN Films that produced series such as '30 for 30' to celebrate its 30th anniversary. It also enabled ESPN to directly compete with HBO Sports, who had a reputation for producing quality television programming. The '30 for 30' documentary series included instalments such as 'Black Magic', which explored the civil rights movement in the context of basketball being played at historically black colleges and universities. The series also pulled in high-profile directors such as Spike Lee to provide a cinematic gravitas to its sports documentaries. This strategic turn towards the sports documentary has been further reinforced by streaming services, which have used the ESPN logic that it can help to compensate for more low-brow programming on the platform. For example, Netflix acquired the distribution rights to 'Icarus', a film about Russian state-sponsored doping that won an Oscar for Best Documentary Feature in 2017 (Vanek Smith, 2018). Sports has also featured heavily in the Sky Documentaries series in the UK, with programmes such as 'The Day Sports Stood Still', about the impact of the COVID-19 pandemic on athletes' lives, while Sky Sports has regularly run in-depth analyses of social issues, such as 'Outraged: Football's Discrimination' that involved interviews with sports stars on racism, sexism and homophobia. This increased interest towards the sports documentary has created fertile conditions for the emergence of the athlete sports journalist.

The rise of athlete sports journalism

The life of a professional athlete is relatively short, with many retired by their mid-30s, leaving them in a position in which they may be wondering what to do with the rest of their life. Some athletes will go into coaching or management, while others find that the media present a viable post-playing career path. Here, retired athletes offer opinion and punditry both in the commentary box and the TV studio during screened sports events. Boyle (2006) notes that in the UK the emergence of the retired athlete-turned-TV pundit can be traced to ITV's coverage of the 1970 World Cup. As the TV sports media expanded exponentially due to the advent of satellite television and a deregulated broadcast sports industry, the opportunities for ex-athletes to be employed as pundits increased (Boyle, 2006).

The print sports media reflected this televisual development in their own coverage as they also employed big-name sportspeople to give insights into their day-to-day lives. In doing so, news organisations could align themselves with a sporting hero who was adored by legions of sports fans, hoping that they could be converted into media audiences. These sportspeople could be paid six-figure annual retainers simply for having weekly conversations with sports journalists, who would then convert the conversation into a column piece. For sportspeople, the opportunity to appear regularly in a national newspaper helped to raise their profile and build their personal brand. However, it was also a useful source of supplementary income at a time when professional sportspeople did not earn enormous sums of money. However, as sports became hyper-commercialised in the 1990s, sportspeople had less financial need to appear in either their local or national newspaper (Boyle, 2006).

Boyle (2006) argues that punditry, "while not strictly journalism ... has become an important part of the wider journalistic discourse that surrounds sport" (p. 74) and makes a distinction between sports journalism and sports broadcasting. These are essentially along the lines of sports journalists providing the objectivity and neutrality, while pundits provide the reaction and chatter around the event. However, the boundaries have blurred between journalist and pundit in the digital age. Smith and Whiteside (2021), in their study of former athletes who enter sports media in the US, argue that the intense competition among all forms of sports media in the digital age has led to finding innovative and attention-grabbing ways of storytelling that are different, new and connect with audiences. An essential part of this strategy is to effectively deploy ex-athletes as doing recognisably journalistic work. Smith and Whiteside (2021) describe it as a process in which sports media organisations "continually reimagine what makes a competent and successful sports reporter or broadcaster; thus reporters like Jim Hill and other former collegiate athletes … could provide a new lens for storytelling and strategy for capturing an audience" (p. 221).

Significantly, the athlete journalist is not merely engaged in the chatter and gossip around sport but is also being given hard-news assignments. Here, the athlete journalist can use their positionality to provide greater depth and insight into the issue. For example, the British Broadcasting Corporation (BBC) in the UK mobilised one of its Premier League pundits, Alan Shearer, a former England captain known for his heading ability, to front a documentary on concussions. Further, former Queens Park Rangers defender Anton Ferdinand, who was the victim in an on-pitch incident that resulted in Chelsea's John Terry being acquitted in a law court but found guilty by the Football Association (FA) of using racist language, explored racism in football in another documentary called 'Anton Ferdinand: Football, Racism and Me', which was produced by Wonder TV and screened on the BBC (BBC, 2020b). Ferdinand received industry recognition, winning the Best Television/Digital Documentary at the Sport Journalists' Association (SJA) Awards 2020. The SJA judges pointed to Ferdinand's own positionality and experiences as leading to a piece of powerful journalism by stating, "The winner showed a different and personal angle to a story well-documented. It was an impactful piece of reflective television that moved the story forward" (SJA, 2021). The BBC's interest in running documentaries that utilise ex-sportspeople's positionality has also expanded into sports beyond football, with former Wales rugby union star Gareth Thomas revealing what life is like living with HIV (BBC, 2019a).

Athletes-turned-journalists have not been confined purely to sports issues. Former England and Arsenal striker Ian Wright presented a BBC documentary on the impact of children growing up in a psychologically abusive and violent home and used his own formative experiences to inform the documentary. Here, Wright made the link to football as providing a release, but his childhood experiences had also led to much unchanneled aggression on the pitch (Wright, 2021). The confessional genre in the UK is not confined to public-service broadcasting or former athletes either, as Sky Sports aired a documentary in May 2021 about current England rugby union player Joe Marler's battle with depression and journey to rebuild his mental health (Sky Sports, 2021b). The programme was called 'Big Boys Don't Cry', which also served as a riposte to toxic masculinity in professional sport. Athlete sports journalism is not purely a UK phenomenon, either. In the US, soccer's Megan Rapinoe, who was player of the tournament at the 2019 Women's World Cup, hosted an HBO sports show called 'Seeing America with Megan Rapinoe', which involved conversations about social change. Rapinoe, a notable athlete-activist who has advocated for equal pay for female soccer players, launched a lawsuit against the US Soccer Federation over gender discrimination and pushed for LGBTQ rights and marriage equality (Zornosa, 2020). Like with Ian Wright's documentary, this was a non-sports-specific programme as it included general discussion involving guests, who were politician Alexandria Ocasio-Cortez, comedian Hasan Minhaj and New York Times investigative reporter Nikole Hannah-Jones, who won a Pulitzer Prize for her work covering civil rights and racial injustice.

Athlete sports journalism has also featured in the BBC's flagship investigative television programme, 'Panorama'. The former 110-metres hurdler Colin Jackson explored eating disorders in 'Sport's Hidden Crisis' and spoke from his own experiences. The programme also contained a healthy dose of holding power to account as Jackson interviewed Dame Katherine Grainger, chair of UK Sport (the Government arm that oversees elite sport), and asked what the authorities were doing about the issue. That said, the emergence of the athlete sports journalist is not to the exclusion of the old-fashioned objective investigative journalist in sport. In 'Boxing and the Mob', screened in February 2021, Darragh MacIntyre interrogated the role of the head of Europe's biggest drug cartels in the proposed heavyweight boxing fight between Tyson Fury and Anthony Joshua (BBC, 2021). MacIntyre has also previously investigated the then head of Formula One motor racing, Bernie Ecclestone, in 2014 (BBC, 2014) along with many non-sports issues, including co-presenting a six-part series about The Troubles in Northern Ireland (BBC, 2019b). There is a distinction to be made here, then, between the BBC's use of athlete sports journalists to explore social issues that chime with their own experience and more traditional investigative journalists to delve into the shadier and more dangerous aspects of sport, such as corruption and wrongdoing.

The sports journalism profession has tended to be less accepting when it comes to ex-athletes making forays into print, rather than broadcast, journalism. Here, former athletes can be accused of poachers turned gamekeepers and can be shunned, at least initially. Mike Atherton, a former England cricket captain is now the chief cricket writer for *The Times* in the UK. However, when Atherton started his career in journalism he was met with the quiet treatment from pack journalists who recalled him being less than co-operative with journalists during his playing career (Turberville, 2018). Soon, though, Atherton was to be accepted by the sports journalism community and won the Sports Journalist of the Year award at the British Press Awards in 2010, when he was hailed by judges for the "brilliance of his writing" (Praverman, 2010). Another discursive device that sports journalists use to condemn ex-athletes crossing this boundary line has been to accuse them of a conflict of interests (Boyle, 2006). The narrative here is that ex-athletes cannot possibly be objective journalists because of their own position within the professional sport system.

Atherton is a sports journalist who produces his own copy. However, a recent trend in UK sports journalism has seen former footballers carry out interviews that are then bylined in the newspaper or its associated website. For example, former Arsenal player and current television pundit Martin Keown, who is used by the *Daily Mail* as a columnist, conducted an in-depth, sit-down interview with his former team-mate, Dennis Bergkamp (Keown, 2020). This prompted a social media debate among sports journalists with one, John Richardson, tweeting, "Sorry don't like this growing fashion of sports stars supposedly interviewing other sports stars in the newspapers. It's already rife in TV and an insult to the many journalists who have painstakingly worked their way up the ladder after proper training". However, a *Daily Mail* journalist, Ian Ladyman, replied, "… they are a valued addition to what we do. Bottom line is that someone like Keown can get to Bergkamp whereas I cannot … They are used to supplement the many interviews done by myself and others for the paper". However, unlike with Mike Atherton and cricket, Keown's interview was recorded by another journalist, Kieran Gill, and written up. While ghost written columns and autobiographies are long-standing and accepted practices in sports journalism, ghost written interviews and features are an unfamiliar development. The *Daily Mail* used a similar approach when former Celtic striker Chris Sutton, another columnist, interviewed Henrik Larsson at a Radisson Blu hotel, again, "while Kieran Gill listens in" (Sutton, 2019). Another UK newspaper, *The Telegraph*, utilised a similar tactic in running a feature that involved Sky Sports pundit Jamie Carragher interviewing former Liverpool team-mate Steven Gerrard. Carragher, like Keown and Sutton, was bylined

(Carragher, 2018). The feature even started with Gerrard asking Carragher, "After some big scoop then are yer?", while Carragher himself muses, "As the tape recorder starts, I have to admit it feels strange. This is not so much an interview as an Anfield (Liverpool's stadium) reunion".

Former athletes conducting interviews and receiving bylines in legacy media are not professional journalism's only concern in this area. In 2015, former New York Yankees player Derek Jeter was part of a consortium that launched The Players' Tribune, which allows athletes to select their own stories and communicate directly with fans while using the branding of legacy media to provide credibility and authenticity. As Schwartz and Vogan (2017) note, the website attached journalistic roles to its athlete writers. This bypassing of legacy media altogether is further undermining sports journalists' role as gatekeepers. It also impacts on sports journalists' access as it means that athletes have even less incentive to stop and talk to reporters and, like team media, news organisations may also be perceived as competitors to The Players' Tribune. Athletes will consider that they have an opportunity to convey unfiltered messages directly to audiences without their words being twisted and manipulated by journalists. However, it means that athletes invariably set their own news agenda and can avoid accountability and scrutiny by an independent journalist.

Even within television sports journalism there are competing claims to authority by both ex-professional athletes who now work ostensibly as pundits and the journalists who are charged with finding and presenting the news. Smith and Whiteside's (2021) interviews with former sportspeople now working in the media reveal that they believed their athlete background enhanced their reporting and storytelling skills, for example through building sources, showing empathy and athlete background. However, Smith and Whiteside (2021) also note that conflicts of interest could undermine their professional credibility while, "among the many advantages the former athletes in this study stated they brought to the table, none included the ability to cast a critical eye toward teams, athletes, and sports organizations" (p. 238).

The notion of former athletes entering into firm sports journalism territory raises questions about the link between experience and expertise. However, this is nothing new. The US journalist George Plimpton employed the reverse tactic, where the journalist becomes a professional athlete. Plimpton chronicled his experiences of playing for the gridiron team Detroit Lions, as a netminder with the National Hockey League (NHL) team the Boston Bruins, as a pitcher in a baseball all-star game and playing on the Professional Golf Association (PGA) tour, among others. For Plimpton, these forays into the arena that he was writing about made him a better journalist because he could better understand the experiences of athletes. However, Steen (2007) notes that Plimpton's writings could lack awareness of social issues. In 1973–74, Plimpton tracked Hank Aaron in his chase of Babe Ruth's 714 home runs, but in his feature, called 'Final Twist of the Drama', for Sports Illustrated, "yet nowhere, remarkably, is there any mention of the agonies Aaron endured en route, chiefly the poison-pen letters and death threats from racists who believed a black man had no right to usurp the mighty Babe (Ruth)" (Steen, 2007, p. 133). Warner (2016) muses on Plimpton's participatory journalism exploits by stating:

> It's sort of impossible to imagine a writer getting as intimate with athletes today as Plimpton was able. Now, our top athletes are mini, or not so mini, corporations, and the 24-hour sports news cycle seems to punish even moderate displays of personality.

However, when journalists have been able to get close to the inside track of sports, there have been accusations of lack of criticality. For example, *The Sunday Times* journalist David Walsh spent three months with cycling's Team Sky in 2013, which led to the book, *Inside Team Sky*. Walsh was a lauded sports journalist who was praised for his work in exposing the doping of the US rider Lance Armstrong, who had won the Tour de France on seven occasions. Team Sky wanted to show Walsh they were clean and wanted him to offer insights into what they described as 'marginal gains' – technical expertise that would give them a competitive edge. Team Sky later suffered a loss of reputation in that they were considered to have exploited the World Anti-Doping Agency's Therapeutic Use Exemption (TUEs) process, whereby athletes can be administered banned substances if there is a medical need. Investigative journalist and former cyclist Paul Kimmage, a long-time friend of Walsh's who had worked alongside him on investigations into Armstrong, accused Walsh of letting his celebrity affect his journalistic judgment and the pair fell out (Kimmage, 2016). Walsh later argued that he had never been told about the TUEs and that he had been "duped" by Team Sky boss Sir Dave Brailsford (BBC, 2017).

Conclusion

Former athletes have long had a close working relationship with sports broadcasting, which has mainly involved punditry but can also involve more substantive, front-facing roles, such as presenting. Former

Arsenal goalkeeper Bob Wilson was a sports presenter with the BBC, while ex-England striker Gary Lineker has fronted the flagship football highlights show, 'Match of the Day', since 1999. Boyle (2006) notes that in Wilson's autobiography he reveals his inside knowledge helped him overcome his difficult beginnings in television. The 'insider' discourse has always been an important one for former athletes seeking to gain legitimacy and credibility in journalistic or broadcasting roles. This chapter demonstrates that, in the digital age, athlete involvement with the media has become more journalistic in nature, whether that be in conducting investigative journalism on television or producing bylined interviews for newspaper websites. This has led to fierce, discursive debate about the nature of journalistic expertise, usually involving contestations of the competing values of objectivity and subjectivity. The need for media organisations to stand out on digital platforms has been a key motivator in mobilising athletes, who are often recognisable, high-profile names, to conduct journalistic work. However, there are other factors, such as the cultural turn on television towards sports documentaries and the move towards more subjective and confessional journalism that is reflective of social media culture.

The response of sports journalists appears to be a rather conflicted one. On the one hand, sports journalists adopt a defensive position in which they can feel undermined. The danger here is that a sports journalist adopts an increasingly passive experience where they watch two former professional athletes have a conversation and record it as a journalistic interview. Further, such 'soft' interviews are unlikely to lead to difficult questions being asked. Certainly, there is evidence, such as the Carragher interview, that the ex-athlete feels that they are 'playing' at being a journalist. The counter-argument here is that journalists see this content as supplementary to their own practices and can find peace with the claim that they would not have been able to source the interview anyway. Further, the fact that the athlete-journalist is on friendly terms with the interviewee can have a disarming effect and lead to greater insight and a more revealing piece of journalism.

Athletes' claim to insider knowledge is a similar discourse on expertise to traditional journalism. A traditional journalist's access to professional sport cannot compete with someone who has either played it or continues to play it, has experienced the locker/dressing room, is friends or acquaintances with key sources and has performed on the field of play. The objectivity norm therefore becomes an important discourse for traditional sports journalists in emphasising their importance over athletes. Ultimately, sports journalists should embrace the increasingly significant contribution of athletes and former athletes in illuminating social issues and using their positionality to inform investigations rather than feel threatened by it. They are providing a different perspective that is contributing to a more multi-layered sports journalism and sits alongside traditional notions of sports journalism rather than displacing it.

6 The Athletic

Prior to the digital age there was a taken-for-granted assumption that sports journalism was the domain of recognised, mainstream news organisations. However, a digital start-up backed by venture capital, called The Athletic, has further complicated and challenged the definitions of who is entitled to practice sports journalism and which organisations count as legitimate employers. The Athletic has recruited sports journalists from both national and local legacy media in the US and the UK during the past five years, mainly through offering large salaries and equity/share options.

The Athletic propounds an original and ambitious subscription-based business model that excludes advertising, unlike other news organisations, and applies a Silicon Valley ethos to sports journalism. To make this model work, The Athletic needs to convince sports fans that its website is worth paying for, in comparison to the sports content that is freely available. Certainly, in the UK, this is a significant undertaking as sports journalism has not meaningfully existed as a specialist format away from a general news product since the 19th century (Boyle & Haynes, 2009; Domeneghetti, 2017). The Athletic's business strategy is based on the ability to sell so-called quality, in-depth and long-form sports journalism, which is counter to the mainstream media's approach to digital platforms that has largely prioritised quantity, brevity and speed. The Athletic is therefore taking different approaches to both professional discourse and practice to distinguish itself from legacy news organisations and create a market position.

The Athletic's disruptive business model

The Athletic launched in the US in 2016, expanded to the UK in 2019 and was employing 430 journalists by March 2020 (Strauss, 2020). Co-founders Alex Mather and Adam Hansmann have a

DOI: 10.4324/9781003106869-6

background, not in journalism, but with the fitness-tracking app Strava. The Athletic's subscription-based, advertisement-free business model has led to it being described as the "Netflix of sportswriting" (Franklin-Wallis, 2020). The Athletic caused consternation in the journalism industry due to its aggressive recruitment strategy to directly approach sports journalists and lure them away from legacy news organisations using high salaries and equity options (Draper, 2018). The Athletic then required its newly recruited sports journalists to conduct rhetorical justification over their moves using introductory pieces that also try to convince their audiences that the site is worth dipping into their pockets for. Sports journalists are then expected to heavily promote their work on social media, even though their work is behind a paywall and they are unable to share it freely.

From the outset, The Athletic made clear its intent to disrupt legacy news media and adopted some of the punk and subversive discursive strategies that we more commonly associated with alternative media such as Deadspin. Mather is quoted in *The New York Times* as saying, "We will wait every local paper out and let them continuously bleed until we are the last ones standing ... we will suck them dry of their best talent at every moment", although The Athletic has since apologised for the comment (Draper, 2017; Franklin-Wallis, 2020). The Athletic's vision is to create a network of local coverage underpinned by an over-arching, national perspective. The Athletic exploited the trend of shrinking national salaries and the low pay of local and regional press as well as newsroom redundancies and lay-offs. The Athletic exercised its financial muscle as "vultures picking over the carcass of once-noble outfits" to signify its arrival as a major media player (Redford, 2017).

The Athletic declared a commitment to sports journalism at a time when it was feeling rather unloved by the news industry. Franklin-Wallis (2020) states: "For once, in an industry that for years had been essentially telling writers their work was worthless, here was somebody trying to show that their work had value, that they had value". The Athletic's US site was launched in 2016, focusing on major league and college sports. Its beginnings coincided with a difficult period for sports journalists in US legacy news media. Fox Sports had dismissed its writing staff as it pursued a video-first online presence (Kalaf, 2017), *ESPN The Magazine* had stopped its print edition, while *Sports Illustrated*, Yahoo and Vice Sports had made sports staff redundant (Franklin-Wallis, 2020; Glasspiegel, 2017; Strauss, 2020). The Athletic targeted sports reporters with significant Twitter followings, which it hoped would convert into subscriber numbers (Buzzelli, Gentile, Sadri

& Billings, 2020). It appointed Sports Illustrated Group's former editor-in-chief Paul Fichtenbaum to be chief content officer (Schmidt, 2017) and lured high-profile sportswriters such as ice hockey's Pierre LeBrun, of ESPN, and baseball's Ken Rosenthal, of Fox Sports (Strauss, 2020). However, it struggled to gain a foothold in key sports areas such as Washington DC, with failed attempts to lure sportswriters from the highly respected *Washington Post* (Wagner, 2018).

In 2019, The Athletic expanded into the UK, focusing on all 20 Premier League football clubs, five Championship sides, the Scottish League, German Bundesliga and women's football (Franklin-Wallis, 2020). Key to this strategy was UK interest in US sport and US interest in UK sport. Here, The Athletic was seeking to capitalise on the globalisation of televised sports, as "U.K. fans of the NBA can watch virtually every single match live on Sky Sports or via NBA League Pass, while foreign supporters of English fourth division soccer clubs can stream all games live" (McCaskill, 2019). The Athletic's UK recruitment strategy had similar mixed results to the US experience. It was able to attract leading local reporters such as Phil Hay, who had covered Leeds United for *The Yorkshire Post*, and top national sports journalists including Daniel Taylor, the chief sports reporter at *The Guardian*. However, The Athletic did not have it all its own way. It claimed that it could not compete with the salaries of the highest paid sportswriters in the UK press, such as *The Times*' Henry Winter and *Daily Mail*'s Martin Samuel (Franklin-Wallis, 2020), and was reportedly rebuffed by others such as *The Daily and Sunday Telegraph*'s Sam Wallace and *The Independent*'s Jonathan Liew (Reynolds, 2019). One senior sportswriter who rejected an offer from The Athletic reflected industry concerns over long-term viability by saying: "They have a big ball of money and they're chucking it around now. It'll only be great if in two years' time there aren't a bunch of great football writers out of work" (Di Stefano, 2019). As The Athletic was attempting to assemble staff in preparation for launch, BuzzFeed laid off 200 journalists in January 2019, leading to increased wariness in the UK of the digital start-up model (Waterson, 2019).

By January 2020, The Athletic had raised $139.5 million of venture capital funding, with backers including the Hollywood actor Matthew McConaghey, and was valued at around $500 million (Fischer, 2020a). In September 2020, The Athletic announced 1 million global subscribers (Sherman, 2020). The aims and motives of the start-up have been the subject of speculation in the industry press, with suggestions that the company exists to be sold (Strauss, 2020). Fox, ESPN, the Sinclair Broadcast Group and Comcast have been mentioned as potential future buyers (Strauss, 2020). The Athletic's presence and business model has had a knock-on effect for sports journalists within legacy media organisations. It helped to shift the market rate for leading sports journalism in that, "It has even managed to raise the salaries of writers it hasn't had – one ESPN writer doubled their salary – more than $500,000" (Strauss, 2020). Vacancies were created within legacy media owing to the departures to The Athletic with, for example, Liew joining *The Guardian*. The Athletic has also changed the professional ambitions and career trajectories of sports journalists in the way that local newspapers will become a "training ground for The Athletic to offer a more lucrative contract" (Buzzelli, Gentile, Billings & Sadri, 2020, p. 1515).

The Athletic has not only helped to cement 'the paywall' as a news business model that applies to quality content but it has shown that specialist journalism can be disembedded from the rest of the news product. While US audiences are used to a specialist sports press, UK consumers have associated sports journalism with a general mainstream press for more than a century (Boyle & Haynes, 2009). However, The Athletic has made a judgment call that the digital environment has led to sections breaking away from the overall offering as "readers are abandoning the entire news bundle for a single section of the paper" (Buzzelli, Gentile, Billings & Sadri, 2020, p. 1517). The Athletic is not alone in this strategy either, as the vertical subscription model becomes increasingly popular within legacy media. For example, national news organisation *The Daily Telegraph* in the UK offers an annual subscription to only its sports section for half the price of accessing all its content, while there are similar local models also emerging, such as for *The Portsmouth News* and *Sheffield Star*. This approach is also happening in the US, with *The Dallas Morning News* and *Miami Herald* among those adopting this strategy. In summer 2020, local news media groups across the US took a 'stronger together' approach in combining to launch a networked, aggregated site, called The Matchup, that collated their content in one place so they could effectively become 'national' (Local Media Consortium, 2020). This collaboration, supported by funding from the Google News Initiative, also enabled content sharing to bolster their individual local news sites.

The Athletic's journalists get to (rhetorical) work

The Athletic's new hires found that they needed to do much more than simply produce quality sports journalism. They took to social and digital media not only to promote their work on the new site but to justify why they chose to leave established legacy media for the relative insecurity and instability of a digital start-up. The Athletic's sports journalists are required to produce an introductory blog when they arrive, which is prefixed with the statement, "Why I joined The Athletic". These blogs are essentially defined by professional issues, with the implication that the only way sports journalism can escape its toy department reputation is if a new entrant arrives in the field, providing a clean sweep of the broom. The Athletic is practically using a crowd-sourcing narrative in that its sales pitch suggests that for this 'breath of fresh air' to succeed, sports fans need to financially support it by taking out a subscription. Here, The Athletic invokes a nostalgic ideal of literary writing in sports journalism that the mainstream media are considered to have abandoned in its pursuit of clicks. Strauss (2020) describes The Athletic as "both a disrupter and a nod to the past" in that it contains "a bundle of local sports section from a healthier era". Clavio and Moritz (2021), in their analysis of introductory pieces in The Athletic, argue that "For a digital platform that is ostensibly forward-thinking about the future of sports media, the definition of what sports journalism should be ... is very much rooted in the past, within the print tradition of journalism" (p. 15). Sports journalists mobilised the professional principle of autonomy as a key justification in why they joined The Athletic (Clavio & Moritz, 2021). Sports writers essentially argued that they had been liberated from mainstream media, where their creativity had been restrained, and their true journalistic prowess would now get the opportunity to flourish. Sports journalists also connected professional logic to the business model in propounding the idea that the mainstream media's pursuit of digital advertising revenue had led to a lowering of standards. The subscription-only model meant that The Athletic was free from commercial constraints and conflicts and could therefore pursue 'good' sports journalism of higher cultural worth and value. Clavio and Moritz (2021) argue:

> The Athletic is portrayed by most of the writers as a platonic ideal of sports journalism, a place free from deadline pressure, clickbait stories, invasive advertisements, editors that want the writer to take the extra time to write the important story, and a focus on writing to the most passionate sports fans rather than the casual consumer.
> (Clavio & Moritz, 2021, p. 15)

The Athletic's definition of quality appears to be sports journalism without advertisements. The emphasis here is on "quality writing and unique storytelling over basic nuts and bolts reporting" (Buzzelli, Gentile, Sadri & Billings, 2020, p. 5). Here, readers as an imagined community were let down by the journalistic standards of their commercial pursuits and they were getting what they deserved with The Athletic – depth and quality (Clavio & Moritz, 2021). The business model of paywall and subscription is aligned with an editorial strategy of quality journalism that is worth paying for. Clavio and Moritz (2021) note that "these columns serve as a way for journalists to define what is proper sports journalism – which is the ultimate sales pitch for The Athletic" (p. 211).

The repositioning of sports journalism within a digital start-up has also brought a 'Silicon Valley' ethos to professional working conditions (Strauss, 2020). Strauss (2020) reports on working conditions as follows:

> A dashboard tracks how stories perform against expectations, and every writer gets goals for how many subscribers their articles should convert. A corporate travel system spits out the average cost of hotels and provides Amazon gift certificates to employees who book cheaper accommodations.
>
> (Strauss, 2020)

The Athletic also employs data analysts who discuss writers' performance in terms of tangible, data-driven metrics that reveal how readers engaged with stories and how much of it they read. Readers can rate articles as "Meh", "Solid" or "Awesome" (Franklin-Wallis, 2020). The Athletic is therefore using a broadly similar commercial logic to legacy media on digital platforms – that each story must gain views to justify its existence and that there is a need to produce more of the better-performing content. As Boudway (2019) notes:

> Feedback loops aren't always kind to journalists, who want to believe that readers care about finely turned phrases, hard-won insights, and nuanced portraits. But traffic data show that what many want are rumors about where free agents are going to sign, reminders about what time the Super Bowl starts, and opinions about whether, if LeBron James had a time machine, he could beat Michael Jordan one-on-one.
>
> (Boudway, 2019)

The outcome of these metrics could potentially impact on sports writers' claims that they have professional freedom to pursue stories. Further, it raises issues of whether the discourse of 'quality' journalism becomes synonymous with popularity. Dowling and Vogan (2015) argue, "digital longform features often operate as loss leaders for their parent companies ... they do not directly generate profits but build a branded sense of symbolic capital that leads to economic profits in less direct ways" (p. 211). However, brand building can only take things so far when your business model places long-form journalism at its centre. A metrics-driven approach could potentially lead to a narrow news agenda and a homogeneity of content as news organisations focus on the types of stories that play well with audiences. Under this model, long-form journalism only has a future if a critical mass of subscribers read it. There is a danger that a metrics and data-driven approach can still lead to clickbait journalism, only without the advertising. Sports writers' claims to a purer approach to sports journalism also jars with The Athletic's expectation that they effectively do sales work in converting their social media followings into subscribers. Following its launch, journalists provided discount codes to their Twitter followers (Franklin-Wallis, 2020). However, sports writers face a significant challenge in maintaining their Twitter followers who are not subscribers as they are promoting links and work that cannot be freely accessed.

The Athletic's arrival has prompted legacy media to defend their own position as the natural home of sports journalism. News organisations must both distinguish themselves from The Athletic while also reassuring audiences that sports journalism's future is still with legacy media rather than digital start-ups. Buzzelli, Gentile, Sadri & Billings (2020) interviewed editors at legacy news organisations in North America to see how they had responded to The Athletic. Some editors considered The Athletic to be situated within a different space in the sports journalism field in that it "caters specifically to hardcore fans willing to pay money for additional content – different than the casual fans who gravitate to their local newspaper's website" (p. 9). Far from condemning The Athletic as an upstart, editors saw the site as a positive because it "helps the general public buy into the idea that quality content comes at a price" (pp. 13–14).

Editors also combated The Athletic using various discourses. One claimed that significant Twitter followings were not an indicator of a good journalist. The editor stated: "... the writers they get generally are Twitter celebrities, as opposed to actually good journalists ... a Twitter celeb who pushes buttons and that's it" (Buzzelli, Gentile, Billings & Sadri, 2020, p. 1522). Also, the intensified multimedia practices that characterise digital sports journalism were articulated as professionally desirable. One editor asked a writer, "do you want to have a byline every day? Or do you want to have a byline once a week"

(Buzzelli, Gentile, Billings & Sadri, 2020, p. 1522), while another editor offset the fact that The Athletic would produce one story from a hockey practice while his news organisation would "have four posts and two videos" (Buzzelli, Gentile, Billings & Sadri, 2020, p. 1523). Editors also compared The Athletic's uncertain and unproven business model against the stability and history of legacy media, even though frequent lay-offs and redundancies persist. Their attempts to persuade sports journalists who had been approached by The Athletic to stay was based on "regular work, ability to travel to road contests, stability, and brand" (Buzzelli, Gentile, Billings & Sadri, 2020, p. 1522). Sports journalists who remained with legacy media have attempted to weaponise media access to exclude The Athletic and protect their boundaries. Franklin-Wallis (2020) states: "When The Athletic first landed, some press packs, including at England internationals, supposedly tried to freeze its reporters out, frustrated by a tendency to ask detailed questions about technical minutiae".

Thinking outside the press box: The Athletic and professional practice

There is debate about whether The Athletic has delivered on its discursive claims to quality journalism or is simply dressing up standard practices and the "familiar mixture of rumours, myth-making, puffery and sporadic insight, only at far greater expense" (Robson, 2019). Redford (2017) argues that the rhetoric does not match the reality as The Athletic "sell what is essentially an evolution of the existing model of sports journalism as a paradigm-shattering breakthrough". There are clear strategic ambitions to be different to legacy media, such as not carrying match reports and live blogs, with reporters instead producing a recap piece (Franklin-Wallis, 2020). Journalists must also produce three stories each week, which is a much lower productivity expectation compared to legacy media. The Athletic's rejection of match reports is a notable break from tradition as this format has been a basic function of sports journalism. Bradshaw (2020) states that, for The Athletic, the match report is "an oddity, an antique, and an irrelevance for those who have seen the goals, followed the game on Twitter, and heard the post-match interviews" (p. 7). However, The Athletic still values the notion of journalists being at the sports event. UK editor-in-chief Alex Kay-Jelski stated:

> We do go to football matches, but we are writing analysis pieces, such as speaking to people about a player or finding a news line

which isn't out there, or even using stats and graphics to tell a different kind of story. On top of that we try to do lovely features and interviews as well as featuring comment and analysis of different issues in the game.

(Houghton, 2019)

The Athletic still considers the traditional values of insider access and contacts building to be important to its sports journalism. UK media commentator Ian Burrell notes that "The Athletic's gamble is based on hiring not just long-read football specialists but dogged 'beat' reporters with impeccable training ground contacts" (Burrell, 2019). Further, The Athletic is interested in breaking news, just like any other news organisation. The Athletic made a major statement when its reporters, Ken Rosenthal and Evan Drellich, revealed in 2019 that baseball team Houston Astros were stealing the signs that a pitcher makes to a catcher to indicate the type of ball that he is about to throw using a strategically placed camera on the field of play (Rosenthal & Drellich, 2019). Players or team staff on the sidelines could then indicate to their batter what delivery was coming next by using audio indicators, such as camera. These actions, known as "sign stealing" are against Major League Baseball (MLB) rules so there is a significant public interest to this story, particularly as a league investigation found that the Astros had employed such tactics in the 2017 season when they won the World Series. Rosenthal and Drellich's work was a triumph for good old-fashioned sports journalism in that they sourced the story from Mike Fiers, who was an Astros pitcher in 2017. Rosenthal then became the moral authority on his own story by giving TV interviews, such as on Sportsnet's 'Hot Stove', condemning the Astros' behaviour, which helped to further increase both the visibility and the credibility of The Athletic (Charlie Chaplin Big Fan, 2020).

The Athletic may not be reinventing sports journalism but it offers interesting challenges to existing norms. The Athletic's reporters sometimes deliberately do not sit in the press boxes, an approach that was previously unheard of in sports journalism. As Franklin-Wallis (2020) notes, "writers watching a big game with people close to the club has become its own micro-genre on the site". For example, reporter Andy Naylor watched the Newcastle United versus Brighton and Hove Albion match while observing the reaction in the stands of schoolfriends of Brighton defender Dan Burn, who was returning to his native North-East in the UK for the match (Naylor, 2019). This different perspective helps to expand the boundaries of sports journalism practice and offers contrast to the predictable, routinised coverage that is much easier for media managers to control. Further, The Athletic shows a willingness to extend sports journalism's narrow source environment beyond media managers, coaches and athletes and bring newer voices into the sports discourse. It has also shown that it is prepared to spend resources when needed, for example when they flew a reporter to Argentina to interview the family of Emiliano Sala, a footballer who died in a plane crash as he transferred between clubs, and when another journalist was sent to Senegal to watch Liverpool play Manchester City on the television with the family of Liverpool forward Sadio Mane (Franklin-Wallis, 2020). Again, The Athletic has demonstrated a willingness to break from convention that dictates sports events must be viewed from within the privileged confines of the press box. The use of a range of unofficial sources to cover the sports event could potentially lead to more wide-ranging and important, hard-hitting stories with the cultivation of these contacts. James (2020) outlines further examples of serious journalism being produced by The Athletic, as follows:

> Dominic Fifield's piece on Brentford B shone a light on a potentially ground-breaking change in English football. Dom Luszcyszyn's analysis of netminders in the NHL underscored criticism of recruitment in hockey. Andy Naylor's exclusive on Brighton's aborted trip to Dubai highlighted the genuine security concerns Premier League clubs face every day.
>
> (James, 2020)

The Athletic's arrival provides hope that a greater plurality and range of sports coverage may start to develop more broadly as legacy media adapt to The Athletic as a competitive rival. Buzzelli, Gentile, Sadri & Billings (2020) found The Athletic was influencing some editors to produce more long-form journalism in their coverage "to complement their normal day-to-day beat coverage and game recaps" (p. 8). Further, in the US, there were signs that The Athletic's influence was leading to a greater variety of sports news in that some news organisations were now covering High School sport to offer something different to The Athletic's focus on major league and college sports. Buzzelli, Gentile, Sadri & Billings (2020) added, "editors even acknowledged a shift toward a different content model in which clickbait articles and online ad revenues no longer dictate how and what they publish" (p. 9). However, in the UK, The Athletic only covers football (although it does plan to expand into other sports in future), which further entrenches the media's bias to one particular sport to the exclusion of others. The Athletic does at least demonstrate a commitment to women's football in recruiting Katie Whyatt from *The Daily Telegraph* to specialise in this area (Sports Journalists' Association, 2020a). The Athletic's ethos of challenging existing sports journalism convention to stand out in the digisphere and find a distinctive market position has been adopted by other digital start-ups. For example, DK Pittsburgh in the US was launched in 2017 by Dejan Kovacevic, a former newspaper columnist, with a soft paywall mixture of free and subscription-based content. DK Pittsburgh places field work at the core of its philosophy, which is contrary to legacy media's digital trends towards more office-based routines. While being present at the sports event has always been central to sports journalism, DK Pittsburgh takes an intensive approach to the live experience. Kovacevic said: "We want you to feel like you're there with us". "Whether it's home or on the road ... every game, every practice, every everything, everywhere, no matter where it is" (Conte, 2019). DK Pittsburgh takes a Gonzo approach to its coverage in the way that athletes talk directly into smartphones while reporters take photos and shoot video of them walking into the stadium and even buying food to eat. The site, which employs nine full-time and one part-time staff, is prepared to spend lavishly on travel, around $86,000 a year, to fulfil its mission (Conte, 2019).

Conclusion

The Athletic represents a gamble that is likely to determine the future of sports journalism. Certainly, its arrival provided a welcome boost for an occupation that was being de-professionalised by digital business strategies. Strauss (2020) notes that "SB Nation built a sprawling network of low-paid, part-time sportswriters ... the new bosses at Sports Illustrated are hiring part-time contractors to cover pro and college teams, betting it can grow its audience without professional journalists". Here, the sportswriter, as much as anything else, is the product. However, this may be difficult to square when the local beat reporter does not take their access to professional sport with them, as accreditation is granted to the news organisation rather than the individual journalist, which makes them highly replaceable. The Athletic is therefore relying not on their formal and routinised network of contacts but their informal ones to obtain original stories and prove an attractive proposition to subscribers. The Athletic's success will ultimately depend on whether, "in a world where leagues employ their own beat writers, where hobbyist bloggers and podcasters flood the Internet with content, enough fans remain who will pay for coverage from professional sportswriters" (Strauss, 2020).

If The Athletic can make a profitable business out of long-form and deeply analytical sports journalism, then this would be transformative for professional standing in the digital age. The Athletic boasts of reaching subscriber milestones but these are often fuelled and facilitated by regular discounted deals. Buzzelli, Gentile, Billings and Sadri (2020) note that "the subscription price seems too low to be stable … The Athletic may alter its business model by raising the yearly subscription cost—a hypothetical, yet pragmatic potential consequence" (pp. 1525–1526). If The Athletic fails to make its business model work, this could prove considerably damaging for sports journalism in terms of the financial and professional commitment to its news work. Ken Doctor, a media analyst, is quoted as saying, "If the Athletic doesn't succeed, it would have a chilling effect because it would be a lost bet that people will pay for high-quality sports journalism" (Strauss, 2020). This may not only lead to the suppression of pay and conditions, but it could lead to vindication for news organisations that clickbait journalism represents the only financially viable way forward.

The Athletic has offered a new business model of subscriber-only, advertisement-free content and challenges the perceived wisdom that long-form sports journalism is about cultural rather than economic capital. In taking this approach, The Athletic is challenging the perceived wisdom in digital journalism that quantity and brevity of content is the key to commercial success. The Athletic also provides an interesting entry into sports journalism boundary discourse in its claims that the future of the industry resides outside of legacy media and that digital start-ups offer the freedom and autonomy that the mainstream media, in its pursuits of clicks, cannot.

The Athletic's rhetoric invokes sports journalism's nostalgic past from its print origins and suggests the industry's transition to a digital environment has led to a dumbing-down of standards that it is looking to rectify at a cost to subscribers (Clavio & Moritz, 2021). The Athletic is generally seen as an interloper and a disruptor in the industry, despite recruiting many established sports journalists. However, there are already signs that The Athletic is settling in to becoming an accepted part of a mainstream media landscape that is increasingly being polarised into paywalls and free content. The 2020 Sports Journalists' Association Awards in the UK saw The Athletic finish third behind CNN and *The Telegraph* for the Digital Publisher Award. Katie Whyatt won Young Sports Journalist of the Year, while Daniel Taylor was runner-up for both Football Journalist of the Year and Sports Feature Writer of the Year awards. There were also four other nominations for the The Athletic (SJA, 2021). There are positive indications that legacy news organisations are incorporating more long-form journalism to compete with The Athletic, which demonstrates signs of a broader improvement of health in the profession. However, there is also a danger that legacy media will shy away from in-depth, analytical pieces by leaving that side of the business to The Athletic, and will instead display a renewed and focused commitment to clickbait and shorter stories.

Certainly, The Athletic offers opportunities for sports journalists to fulfil their professional ambitions in digital settings in ways that the legacy media has not. However, The Athletic is stretching the boundaries of sports journalism practice without offering a reinvention of its traditions and conventions. The Athletic does not provide a drastic transformation of what sports journalism is but is challenging the conventions and codes surrounding practice. Its novel approach to sources and thinking outside the press box is motivated by the need to find a distinct position in the marketplace that appeals considerably to sports fans. This approach may also lead to a progressive sensibility that involves a willingness to listen to unreported and ignored voices that can provide important challenges to professional sport. Alternatively, a highly granular, metrics-driven approach to sports journalism could lead to less experimentation as the range of stories is narrowed to those which perform well with the analytics. As Pickard and Williams (2014) note, paywalls reinforce the commodification of news and "further inscribe commercial values into newsgathering processes" (p. 207). Similarly, Buzzelli, Gentile, Billings and Sadri (2020) have expressed concerns:

> The Athletic has seemingly sparked a new era of digital journalism, one in which the competitive nature of sports media may no longer be about journalists doing everything in their power to get the scoop on a story or get the most shares on social media. Instead, the competition may soon turn to media outlets valuing subscriber numbers over quality reporting.
> (Buzzelli, Gentile, Billings & Sadri, 2020, p. 1527)

The answer will ultimately be provided by whether The Athletic's brand of quality journalism is sufficiently distinct from legacy news media and plays well with its subscribers. The website may not carry advertising but it still relies on clicks and subscriber engagement with stories as a marker of success.

7 COVID-19 and sports journalism

The British comedian David Mitchell lampooned Sky Sports' coverage of the English Premier League in the TV show 'That Mitchell and Webb Look' in 2006 with a spoof promotional advert in which he dresses up as an over-enthusiastic presenter and urges:

> Watch it all, all here, all the time, forever, it will never stop. The football is officially going on forever. It will never be finally decided who has won the football. There is still everything to play for – and forever to play it in.
>
> (BBC, 2010)

Except, on March 13, 2020, a funny thing happened. The football did stop because of the COVID-19 pandemic. Arsenal manager Mikel Arteta had contracted coronavirus, Chelsea were self-isolating after one of their players, Callum Hudson-Odoi, had returned a positive test while three Leicester City players were undergoing tests after developing symptoms. The Premier League (EPL) and English Football League (EFL) had announced an emergency meeting that day. By this point, European football leagues such as La Liga in Spain, Serie A in Italy and the Eredivisie in Holland were already suspended. And it was not just football. Golf's Players Championship and Formula One's Australian Grand Prix had been cancelled as well. It was a dynamic and rapidly developing situation. At 9.32am, the German football league (DFL) confirmed that the Bundesliga was to be suspended. At 10.06am, news came through that UEFA, the body that runs European club football competitions, had suspended the following week's Champions League and Europa League matches. At 10.41am, the Grands Prix in Bahrain and Vietnam had been cancelled. At 10.43am, the English Football League (EFL) had announced that fixtures were to be suspended and, 21 minutes later, the EPL and Women's Super

DOI: 10.4324/9781003106869-7

League (WSL) were also confirmed to be shutting down. At 11.13am, the English Football Association (FA) announced that the internationals with Italy and Denmark would no longer be happening. That afternoon, news came through that The Masters golf tournament and the London Marathon were being postponed (Bakowski, Goodwin & Fisher, 2020).

As a result of sporting events being either postponed or cancelled, journalists were left in a curious situation whereby they had no games to report on. The previews, the game report, the reaction and the postmortem – the wheels of the story cycle – had stopped. Shemar Woods, the director of digital for sports at *The Philadelphia Inquirer*, was quoted as saying: "We don't have a guidebook on how to cover sports when sports aren't being played" (Tameez, 2020). Sports journalists, so used to being on the road, suddenly found they had to produce stories from home, without the usual routinised sources of information. How did sports journalism respond? The answer is in a myriad of ways. Woods indicated the lull in sports gave the industry with a much-needed opportunity to reflect and allow reporters to focus on other areas that they did not usually have time to do, such as starting a podcast. However, it also provided sports journalists with opportunities to investigate the wider implications of the pandemic's impact on sport in the search for new stories. Woods stated: "The biggest story for me is the guy who was dependent on the Sixers game tonight who won't be able to work – how does that affect him, and how does that impact his family?" he said. "So we're going to be on the ground. We're going to go to the bowling alley. We're going to go check out sports bars as well" (Tameez, 2020).

Sports journalists also explored how sport intersected with government decision-making around the pandemic. For example, in the UK, mass-event sport gatherings still took place despite other European countries being in lockdown. Approximately 3,000 Atletico Madrid fans travelled from Spain, already a COVID-19 hotspot, to attend a Champions League match against Liverpool. Around 54,000 supporters attended this game, which was the last major football contest played in England before all sports activity ceased. David Conn, a sports journalist with *The Guardian*, conducted interviews with some of the fans who were at the match and believe they contracted COVID-19 as a result (Conn, 2020). In his piece, Conn asks searching questions about whether the British Government was too slow to react, knowing that the disease had already taken hold in other countries in Europe. Other sports events that were allowed to go ahead included the England v Wales rugby international in Twickenham on March 7, which the prime minister Boris Johnson had attended, and the Cheltenham Festival, which attracted 260,000 racegoers.

Bradshaw (2020) notes that sports journalists had to turn to good old-fashioned practices, such as working their contacts book, moving away from the reliance on spoon-fed information subsidies within professional sport to come up with stories. Bradshaw (2020) argues that "being stuck at home with the gift of some time on their hands, rather than charging to press conferences and regurgitating a manager's quotes, has allowed some sports journalists to flourish in an alternative habitat" (p. 4). For instance, the *Inishowen Independent* in Northern Ireland covered stories about how families could do exercise while in lockdown, while the sports agency, Associated Press (AP), found they needed to report on sport's response to the pandemic for their clients (Tameez, 2020). Local news journalists could explore the impacts of COVID-19 on the clubs in their communities (Gray, 2020). Other sports media outlets gravitated towards nostalgia and reminiscence, with UK radio station talkSPORT running discussion topics such as "players describing what it meant for them to score goals" and "how much we are missing sports" (Nilsson, 2020).

For some, it was a case of drilling deeper into whatever remained of professional sport. *USA Today*'s sports website, For the Win, covered the NFL free-agency period more thoroughly than they normally would have done (Tameez, 2020). In other quarters it was a rather simple and basic decision – reduce the number of pages and digital space devoted to sport. Sports journalists were seconded to news departments to provide help with the general reporting of the pandemic (Cash, 2020; Tameez, 2020). In the UK, some sports journalists found themselves furloughed. For example, the Press Association placed 44 sports journalists on paid leave while Reach, which published the *Daily Mirror, Daily Express* and *Daily Star* titles, included sports journalists among 940 staff on furlough (Mayhew, 2020b). Mayhew (2020b), writing on the trade website of the *Press Gazette*, quoted a Reach sports journalist as saying, "With no sport, our department has been hit hardest … the back pages have been slimmed down and the online content is threadbare". For other sports journalists, being forced to work from home and away from wider colleagues was a culture shock in a job that thrives on its sociability and human contact (Kelly, 2020).

Freelance sports journalists were particularly affected by the pandemic as they were readily dispensable when news organisations needed to save money (Tameez, 2020). A freelancer said:

> Sports journalists are having to try and be a little bit more creative and think outside the box in terms of content. I think some places

are getting by with less coverage – cutting pagination down for sport to cope with the lack of it.

(Mayhew, 2020b)

However, Reach revealed that its 70 national and regional news websites were seeing more than 10 million page views above average. *Daily Mirror* traffic was up 60 per cent on the previous year and a Reach spokesperson was quoted as saying, "We've also found that the *Daily Mirror*'s football content remains consistently well-read despite the lockdown, so they've been finding different ways to cover it, for example more long reads and interviews" (Mayhew, 2020a).

Back on the beat: Journalism and the return of sport

Following the initial freezing of sport, professional leagues scurried to implement COVID-secure protocols, such as regular testing for athletes, that would allow them to resume under slogans, such as the NHL's Return to Play and the Premier League's Project Restart. Elite professional sport did eventually resume in the middle of 2020 with one significant difference – the omission of fans. Sports journalists were among the few parties who were allowed inside stadiums and arenas. These developments led to a closer identification by media managers of who constituted legitimate media, instantly imbuing admitted sports journalists with heightened credibility and importance. However, sports leagues expected journalists to show sufficient enthusiasm for the return of sport, suggesting a perception of them as 'cheerleaders'. Alex McDaniel, a video strategist at Meredith Corporation, a media and marketing company, sarcastically tweeted, "sports reporters could eradicate this virus if they'd just be more upbeat about it, damn". Frank Pallotta, a media reporter at CNN, tweeted, "The forming narrative that reporters want sports or movies to close is dumb. I can't speak for all of the media, but as a reporter I want pastimes to open, but to do so [in a way] that's safe for all involved." Gregg Doyel, of *The Indianapolis Star*, was critical of the restart by arguing, "we are prioritizing the health of thousands of athletes over the health of millions of the rest of us", contrasting the speed and frequency with which professional athletes were getting tested with the testing shortages and backlogs seen in the general population (Doyel, 2020). Doyel (2020) explained the difficulty of arguing against sport's resumption because his colleagues had been furloughed and his employers were losing tens of thousands of dollars – "Nobody needs sports more than me, a sports writer".

Journalists also needed to hold sport to account in interrogating the motivations of leagues and clubs in making such a swift return to the sporting arena. For instance, Mik Awake, a writer with the New Yorker, accused the National Football League (NFL) of "attempting to survive the pandemic in the way it always has: by banking on the devaluation of Black [lives]" (Awake, 2020). Sport's return still led to disrupted schedules as athletes, coaches and/or other backroom staff continued to test positive for COVID-19. This would present a new ethical dilemma for sports journalists about whether they disclosed the individuals who had been diagnosed with coronavirus. *Miami Herald* sportswriter Barry Jackson tweeted, "The other question flummoxing journalists is whether to identify athletes who tested positive for COVID if the player or his rep does not authorize the release of his name. Most NBA reporters have respected players' wishes. Will be interested to see if NFL writers follow suit". *The Philadelphia Inquirer* reported that the Miami Marlins baseball team decided, through a group text message exchange between players, to proceed with their game against Philadelphia Phillies even though they learned of three positive tests that same morning, including their starting pitcher. Two Phillies players wore face masks during the game (Breen, 2020). Breen (2020) noted: "The Marlins flew together to Philadelphia from Atlanta, traveled by bus to a Center City hotel, traveled by bus to the ballpark, dressed in the clubhouse, and sat in the dugout".

Sports journalists who returned to the beat were also subject to more rigorous screening protocols. Dieter Kurtenbach, a sports journalist with the Bay Area News Group, told The Ringer that in order to return to the San Francisco Giants press box, "I think I gave Rob Manfred (MLB commissioner) rights to my kidney when I walked in there" (Curtis, 2020). However, reporters also recognised that they were making history in covering sport in one-off ways, such as the NBA bubble at Walt Disney World (Kludt, 2020), although fewer reporters were being sent to the event (Mullin, 2020). Reporters could find themselves excluded as the pandemic gave media managers vital room to manoeuvre in omitting journalists. *The Echo*, a daily local newspaper in Essex in the UK, was excluded from an FA Cup tie because its work was considered 'non-essential'. Here, the club were invoking government discourse that determined who was and who was not entitled to travel during lockdown. Instead, *The Echo* chief sports reporter, Chris Phillips, watched the contest between Boreham Wood and Southend United on a live stream provided free by the club (Sports Journalists' Association, 2020b). However, the broadcast sports media, including local radio, were permitted access to the ground. This was not just a regional news issue either, as *The Times* reporter Molly Hudson and *The Guardian* journalist Suzy Wrack were denied access to the Women's Super League (WSL) match between Arsenal and Chelsea, which also took place at Boreham Wood (Sports Journalists' Association, 2020b). *Toronto Star* journalist Kevin McGran wrote an editorial that accused the National Hockey League (NHL) of excluding reporters in favour of their own team media writers (McGran, 2020). McGran stated that the NHL was not allowing reporters to attend practices or morning skates and they were not permitted in the COVID-secure hubs of Edmonton and Toronto. However, McGran stated that three writers from NHL.com and one social media member per team were allowed. One person from each media outlet could watch the team they cover from the stands during a match, when usually four or five writers would attend a Toronto Maple Leafs home play-off game. McGran argued:

> That means any news, reports, feeds, pictures, stories from Hotel X or the Fairmont Royal York or behind the scenes at Scotiabank Arena will be sanitized, NHL- or team-approved versions. So, not real news.
>
> (McGran, 2020)

However, other media organisations decided that they were going to be more cautious in sending sports journalists back on to the beat because of the health risks. For example, Minnesota's *Star Tribune* decided not to send its Minnesota United writer Jerry Zgoda to the Major League Soccer (MLS) Is Back tournament in the summer of 2020 because of Florida's worsening COVID-19 situation at the time (Carr, 2020).

Exclusive access: Sports journalists in empty stadiums

The limited access to arenas and stadiums did, however, have benefits for sports journalists. The fact that a select few individuals were permitted into stadiums and arenas under coronavirus protocols provided a clear boundary between sports journalists and other content producers. This situation has helped to reinforce sports journalists' self-perception that their role is to furnish fans with inside information that only a privileged few experts can access. In this respect, it has enabled sports journalists to provide a timely reminder of their status and importance in a digital era where their status as experts has been questioned.

Sports journalists could enhance their reportage by making a note of sounds and statements from both coaches and players – exchanges that would usually have been drowned out by the noise of crowds. Similarly, the coronavirus protocols forced fans into a greater reliance on mainstream media for their interaction and engagement with sports. Sports journalists could therefore draw more exaggerated attention to their role as eyewitnesses to the sports event. For example, Alasdair Gold, who covers Premier League club Tottenham Hotspur for Football. London, drew attention to such exchanges in his report on the North London derby with Arsenal in March 2021 (Gold, 2021). Tottenham midfielder Erik Lamela had just scored an outstanding goal when Gold chronicled his reaction to his manager, Jose Mourinho, in the immediate aftermath, as follows:

> Lamela yelled at the bench in the aftermath, pointing at Mourinho & Co, delighted that he had shown them that it was worth the wait for him to come on for Son. Mourinho had shouted 'vai, vai, vai' – the Portuguese for 'go, go, go' – at the Argentine as he took his time in getting ready to enter the pitch 20 minutes into the match and Lamela with his roar knew this was the perfect response.
>
> (Gold, 2021)

It is arguable whether sports journalists would be able to access such detailed verbal communication with fans present – much would depend on the proximity of the press box to the field of play at any given stadium – but certainly it is a snippet of information that supporters sitting at home, who are subjected to artificial crowd noise, would not have access to in the mediated spectacle. It is also doubtful whether such reportage is possible in the long-term once stadiums are noisier, but in the short-term it has certainly helped to reinforce sports journalism's notion of 'insider access' as important to expertise, providing fans with details that, even in an age of what Hutchins and Rowe (2012) describe as 'digital plenitude', fans themselves cannot reach or obtain.

The disruption that the pandemic caused has obviously made digital technology, in particular video conferencing software such as Zoom or Microsoft Teams, pivotal in the continued running of businesses and organisations. This has also been the case in professional sport, which used digital technology to reconfigure and redefine the way it related to journalists. While – where permitted – the in-stadium experience has presented sports journalists with opportunities to reinforce their boundaries with fans and signpost their privileged position, the coronavirus protocols surrounding sport events have presented more troubling challenges for journalists that may have longer-term consequences. Because of social distancing, sports journalists have been conducting press conferences via video conferencing software. This interviewing-at-a-distance enables even greater control by media managers, where "access restrictions haven't just persisted ... they've intensified" (Allsop, 2020). This is arguably more keenly felt by US sports journalists where, "instead of getting access to team locker rooms and conducting interviews there, reporters are now forced to request players from the team's PR staff and do streaming interviews" (Moritz, 2020). These developments have raised concerns that the US is moving to a model more commonly associated with the UK, whereby media managers are hand-picking players to present to the media. In the New York Yankees' first work-out after the resumption of spring training, starting pitcher Masahiro Tanaka was taken to hospital after being hit on the head by a baseball from a shot by batter Giancarlo Stanton (Kuty, 2020). However, NJ.com writer Steve Politi described,

> with no clubhouse access, we didn't have a chance to talk to the man who hit the ball, Giancarlo Stanton, or get reaction from the rest of the players. The only interviews were with two team-chosen players and manager Aaron Boone, and those were conducted over a Zoom video conference despite their presence two stories below in the stadium.
>
> (Politi, 2020)

Politi (2020) also warned that "without us poking around, fans are going to be less informed". However, there could be positives to Zoom calls. Godfrey (2020) notes the virtual press conference can be less intimidating for women sports journalists than physical ones, as it removes the "fear of embarrassment, toxicity, or even harassment for reporters on the job ... without an actual physical environment within which to exist, the exuberant masculinity should be less apparent, allowing for a more diverse group of reporters to feel comfortable doing their jobs". Godfrey (2020) also argues that Zoom calls may leave sports journalists more prepared to ask challenging questions – "with an intimidating and sometimes angry athlete standing in a reporter's midst, it can be difficult to truly ask poignant and profound questions out of fear of embarrassment or a hostile response".

The Athletic

The pandemic has provided a specific challenge to specialist sports publications and sites in that they cannot fall back on the other sections of the newspaper or website. However, the Athletic's focus on long-form, contextual stories meant that it could still write about sport even though it was not actually taking place. Bradshaw (2020) argues that The Athletic's configuration and wiring in its relationship with sport meant that COVID-19 impacted on it less than other sports media, "simply because its content is not dictated by – or even built around match reporting" (p. 7). The Athletic's UK editor-in-chief, Alex Kay-Jelski, stated in an interview with the *New Statesman* that, "Our writers worked bloody hard and had to come up with a lot more ideas. We got stuck into nostalgia pieces" (Bannerjee, 2020). One journalist at The Athletic told the *Press Gazette*: "It's different, clearly, now that we don't have the usual weekly rhythms to work around. But it has also been an opportunity to be creative – to try different things and look for stories off the beaten path" (Mayhew, 2020b). Instead of providing coverage of the latest fixture, it is asking readers to "find comfort and entertainment in the nostalgia, culture, and people behind the games we love". In a note to subscribers, The Athletic said it had set up a "#lets-get-weird Slack channel for our 500-plus employees" to brainstorm ideas to replace the daily flow of sports news. Some reader comments posted under the message said they would not pay for sports coverage when no matches were being played (Nilsson, 2020).

While it was editorially resilent, The Athletic was commercially impacted by the absence of sport. Douglas McCabe, media analyst at Enders Analysis, told the *Financial Times*: "If your entire business is sports journalism, this is a challenging period" (Nilsson, 2020). The Athletic co-founder Adam Hansmann said that in the first two weeks after sports shut down in March 2020, "there were days when fewer than 100 people were signing up for The Athletic, compared with 'thousands' normally" (Sherman, 2020). The Athletic normally charges £4.99 a month for subscriptions but started lowering barriers of entry by offering reduced fees and other incentives, such as a limited deal at £2.99 a month in the UK and 90 days free in the US (Mayhew, 2020b). It was also reported that The Athletic had struck a deal to become the official sportsbook partner of BetMGM (Allen, 2021). The agreement would see The Athletic creating a dedicated betting hub that would involve betting content with BetMGM live odds and offers (BetMGM, 2021). The Athletic pointed to such editorial perks as BetMGM making its Vice-President of Trading available for a mailbag feature, offering more content to subscribers and thus providing more value for their outlay, and suggested that the data obtained will "make stories and columns deeper and more insightful … a good betting story is a good story" (Di Fino, 2021). Partnerships between sports betting firms and media organisations in the US have become increasingly common due to the trend of states relaxing their gambling laws (Toonkel and Dolan, 2020). However, such a deal raises important ethical and professional issues. First, there are the social consequences and implications of gambling. Second, such a deal could potentially create conflicts of interests for their journalists and impact on independence and autonomy. Thirdly, it creates ethical questions for the relationship with readers, as such arrangements usually involve audiences being referred to the betting site with the media organisation taking a cut of any revenue that arises. Fourthly, where does this leave The Athletic's commitment to 'pure' sports journalism and an ad-free subscription model going forward?

The Athletic was not immune to the financial pressures wrought upon news organisations by the pandemic. It laid off 46 people, 8 per cent of its workforce, while issuing 10 per cent pay cuts across its staff for the rest of 2020. Among the staff being laid off were Atlanta Falcons writer Jason Butt, Arizona Cardinals writer Scott Bordow, Tennessee Titans writer John Glennon, and LA Lakers and Clippers writer Brett Dawson (Bucholtz, 2020). Joint CEO Alex Mather described the cuts as the last resort after The Athletic had applied "reduced travel, freelance cutbacks, extreme cutbacks on marketing spend, and deep pay cuts for our entire HQ leadership team" (Fischer, 2020b). However, the return of sport also led to a return of The Athletic's fortunes. The 10 per cent pay cut was lifted in mid-October 2020 (Bupp, 2020). It also reached the 1 million subscriber milestone, although this figure included trials or discounted rates (Bannerjee, 2020; Sherman, 2020). The Athletic's UK editor-in-chief, Alex Kay-Jelski, stated: "It was quite scary […] but thankfully when the football came back, so did the interest, and the readers" (Bannerjee, 2020).

Conclusion

COVID-19 initially created a considerable problem for news organisations in that the cessation of sport meant they would struggle to fill the vast digital space that they would usually reserve for such coverage. They responded in different ways, but there was certainly the opportunity to place sports journalists in a position whereby they could demonstrate there was more depth to their reporting ability than had previously been realised. Sports journalists would need to take a more expansive approach to source relations that would lead to them having to generate stories by cultivating contacts who were not the usual official sources. This approach aligned sports journalists more closely to their news counterparts. Further, in some cases, sports journalists were reallocated to the news desk, which, again, gave them the chance to show that they had the same rigorous approach to their job than their wider colleagues.

Upon the return to action, journalists had to navigate some challenging and complex reporting scenarios that required them to closely examine both their own ethics and those of professional sport during the pandemic. Sport provided a centrepiece for reporting on the pandemic in general, both in how it created a site for mass gatherings that could lead to the spread of the coronavirus while also prompting important health and safety considerations for athletes upon the resumption. This also provided further opportunities for sports journalists to demonstrate they were not merely the toy department. To report effectively on sport's return, journalists had to take a critical approach to professional sport while also exercising their independence and professional distance, even though there were often expectations to the contrary among official sources. Sports journalists needed to scrutinise why leagues were so desperate to restart at the height of the pandemic, which was often mainly motivated by fulfilling lucrative TV and sports rights contracts under the auspices of brightening fans' lives in lockdown. They also needed to challenge professional sport on its privileged position and preferential treatment in accessing testing when it was difficult for the public and wider society to do so.

The COVID-19 pandemic disrupted sports journalists' routines in ways that forced them to adapt and do things differently. As sport gradually returns to normal with the end of social distancing and the return of fans, it remains to be seen how many of the new habits that have emerged during the pandemic are retained. Some of these are desirable for the good of sports journalism. As Moritz (2020) notes:

> The pandemic has starved sports journalists of the diet of easy quotes that they can get from press conferences, instead forcing them to go to more challenging places for their quotes and sustenance. This has been liberating for some, unshackling them from the tedium of stage-managed pressers. Let's hope the shackles remain off.
>
> (Moritz, 2020, p. 6)

Equally, though, sports reporters may just slip back into the old habits of relying on heavily routinised, predictable and sanitised official sources of information, which requires little exercising of journalistic faculties. Other adjustments that have happened to the media's relationship with sports are less desirable. Sports clubs and leagues have used the pandemic as an opportunity to limit access further, which in some cases have led to the total exclusion of journalists from the live event. This development has simply heightened and accelerated the trend of sports journalists being forced into increasingly distant reporting from the athletes who they cover. While sports journalists should not be too reliant on this aspect of their jobs, nevertheless, these media briefings and press conferences often provide them with their only opportunity to hold professional sport to account and ask questions. Placing sports journalists at a farther distance to professional sport only serves to make this more difficult. It means that team media become more prominent and can take firmer control of the news agenda, leading to a further softening of the news.

COVID-19 has ultimately contributed to sports journalism's long-standing professional uncertainty and angst, particularly surrounding its future. However, it should force sports journalism to carefully rethink whether it was exercising enough range and variety in its approach to practice prior to the pandemic. Sports journalists also need to contemplate whether their reliance on access to professional sport is sustainable and whether they need to think in different ways about the nature of their sources, and to what extent they become more like news journalists in developing off-diary stories and less cyclical work routines.

8 Conclusion
Future considerations

Sports journalists are facing a battle for professional survival in the digital age as they attempt to distinguish themselves from bloggers, team media and even athletes. Sports journalism can no longer rely on its 'toy department' characteristics of soft news, opinion, bias and partisanship, as these have been appropriated by other actors in different digital spaces. Sports journalists can therefore only locate professional distinctiveness in their 'serious' and 'proper' news work, where they "should be taking advantage of their background to provide superior insights and analyses of their sport, to shape the mediated discourses, and to make connections to day-to-day society" (Lowes & Robillard, 2018, p. 315).

The trajectory of sports journalism in the digital age has been towards de-professionalisation as legacy media have re-oriented the occupation towards digital practices that are office based, clerical and generally involve poor pay and conditions. There have been signs of both digital innovation and a re-working of professional principles in formats such as live blogging (McEnnis, 2016). However, digitally native news work is often characterised by clickbait, triviality and entertainment as news organisations look to produce more content. As Ramon and Tulloch (2019) note, "journalism has been unequivocally affected by the fixation on metrics, the growing inclination towards predictable content, the reliance on public relations material, and the expansion of practices linked to news commodification and tabloidization, such as clickbaiting" (p. 2).

Digital sports journalism also offers a lack of depth and critical edge due to the emphasis on speed. It often involves curation and repurposing content for different platforms rather than story gathering and, while there is the potential to use the internet for networked collaboration in scrutinising power, this is not what news organisations are demanding. This de-professionalisation has been reinforced by the removal of

DOI: 10.4324/9781003106869-8

Conclusion 95

'journalist' from job titles, which tempers both expectations of and requirements for serious news work. News organisations' requirements for populating their digital platforms also have an impact on traditional journalists, who are asked to engage more with transfer rumour and speculation and are encouraged to file stories on fewer teams. The multiple roles and orientations within newsrooms have led to a potential diluting and side-lining of the responsibility for serious and proper sports journalism. The fact that roles such as 'sports news' correspondents now exist in newsrooms has the potentially dangerous effect of absolving the majority of the profession from exercising scrutiny in this way, as it is 'not their job' to deliver hard news and perform serious journalism. This means that serious journalism is not a standard expectation from every sports journalist and suggests that their focus should be more on performing commercial rather than professional functions.

The emergence of The Athletic has disrupted this trend in that this digital start-up offers a renewed economic and cultural commitment to the traditional core values of sports journalism. A wider shift towards subscription-based models of sports content also offers hope that sports journalists will be both empowered by news organisations and strive themselves to produce quality stories that go beyond that which are freely available. The Athletic's entry into a field of competition means that it can also influence legacy media to renew or reinforce their commitment to serious sports journalism. However, these emergent developments are highly contingent and unpredictable. The Athletic faces economic challenges in maintaining a commitment to advertisement-free content and any concession in this area could impact on the autonomy and independence of its journalists. Besides, The Athletic is still a metrics-driven website that can lead to serious journalism being marginalised if it fails to perform commercially. Meanwhile, a subscription-based model of sports journalism still needs to prove its sustainability in a digital news ecosystem that has been defined by instability and experimentation over the past 20 years or so.

The pause and resumption of sport due to COVID-19 has presented opportunities and reminders that sports journalists need to, and can, do the heavy lifting around serious stories. The COVID-19 pandemic has provided new conditions where sports journalists can enhance their authority and demonstrate their commitment to serious journalism. Sports journalists find themselves among the few people allowed inside stadiums, which helps them to re-emphasise their importance as the eyes and the ears of the public. Sports has emerged as an important and serious topic in the pandemic, particularly regarding the moral implications of sport's restart, and has been an important tool in scrutinising the health and safety aspects of leagues claiming to have created COVID-secure environments. Sports journalists have faced challenges in scrutinising the restart, with reasons given being under the guise of lifting the public mood, however, this is underpinned by economic motives, particularly the need to fulfil lucrative broadcasting contracts to prevent leagues' business models from effectively collapsing. However, COVID-19, in leading to sports journalists being some of the few allowed into arenas and stadiums, has provided them the opportunity to further entrench beliefs that they are producers of information for a passive audience, helping to emphasise their cultural importance and significance over fans. However, hopes that sports journalists could take a different attitude to their news work, towards more inclusive and collaborative practices that flatten hierarchies, particularly between themselves and supporters, have not been realised. As Lowes and Robillard (2018) note, "digital media give them the opportunity to ... become actual journalists" (p. 316).

The future of access: All, some or no areas?

There are, ultimately, two forces in play when considering the future of journalists' accreditation to professional sport. Firstly, the trend over the past 25 years has been towards dwindling access to professional sportspeople and the portents are that this development will only worsen as team media becomes increasingly prominent. Sports journalism has been doubling down on accreditation but is now seeing that usurped by in-house team media. Sports journalists have traditionally aligned their expertise with their access to professional sport that provides them with privileged information that occupational outsiders cannot obtain. But this professional base is being shown to be extremely limited and problematic in the digital age.

Secondly, there is the question of whether sports journalists and news organisations reconsider their reliance on professional sport and official sources on stories in their attempts to be distinctive from their rivals. There has already been academic debate around whether sports journalists need to move towards a greater range of sources and listen more to marginalised voices (McEnnis, 2017; Serazio, 2021). Press conferences and briefings are highly visible across television, websites and social media (Lowes & Robillard, 2018), and the homogeneity of content that arises from what limited access there is does not help news organisations to stand out from the crowd in a competitive digital marketplace. Serazio (2021) argues that this continued reliance will only lead to a further deterioration of editorial independence, and therefore quality, so "media might orient themselves to be less in need of access to sports newsmakers, if credentials still come at the cost of deferential acquiescence" (p. 14). Reinforcing this argument, Boyle (2021) states that, "in an age of always-on sports coverage, looking for other journalistic paths to follow to engage the audience should be a more common practice than it is" (p. 356), while Lowes and Robillard (2018) believe that "sport coverage in digital culture offers more opportunities for journalists to step outside the confines of traditional sport-journalism work routines and news-production practices" (p. 309). However, Moritz (2020) argues that access "does matter ... access allows them to build relationships with the players and coaches .... That's fundamental to the way they conceptualize their jobs, whether they're breaking news ... or writing features".

The best answer is likely to be a blended approach towards official and unofficial sources, routinised and non-routinised story gathering, and on-diary and off-diary approaches. Formalised and officially convened press conferences often provide a rare space where sports journalists can offer some semblance of ability to hold power to account, although we do tend to see managers and coaches being forced to speak on behalf of their employers for their morally dubious actions. Further, press conferences and media briefings provide the 'in' into professional sport and a launchpad to potentially develop contacts. As subscription models require sports journalism to be increasingly original and distinctive, this can only be achieved beyond the shackles of media managers and through developing a wider base of sources. Hopefully the lessons learned from reporting in a pandemic will live on and sports journalists will continue to develop a range of sources and sufficient distance from professional sport to enable them to take critical stances and objective positions.

Sports journalism: An evolving professional field?

Sports journalists have adopted a curious blend of passivity and determination in attempting to protect professional boundaries. Sports journalists fiercely protect their core routines, particularly their access to professional sport, from outsiders and interlopers. However, they are content to both allow bloggers into professional contexts while also taking themselves into more amateur modes of production, such as fan podcasts. Sports journalists' move into amateur spaces can either help them to connect with fans better and repoint their allegiances towards the public rather than professional sport, or it can reinforce their hierarchical position and reinforce the myth of insider access. The field of sports journalism can be conceptualised as having porous and weak boundaries that enable different professions, such as financial services and law, to move in and out of it when they, as bloggers, need to provide important information to the public that enriches and expands the democratic contribution. Here, other professional fields can use their expert knowledge to shed light on complex sports issues and engage with legacy media to maximise that audience reach. A porous field provides scope for a milieu of "other interest groups – public service media, independent writers and other emergent subscription-based organizations – to pursue broader agendas and to produce a greater diversity of stories beyond those that simply serve to promote the interests of men's professional sport" (Daum & Scherer, 2018, p. 565). As Forde and Wilson (2018) note, "the apparently burgeoning linkages between academics, activists, and journalists interested in sport-related social issues [seem] to be a promising avenue for change" (p. 73).

These developments involve a blurring of the boundaries between who is and is not a professional sports journalist and what does and what does not constitute sports journalism. This invariably leads to questions concerning whether we need sports journalists at all, seeing as more alternative sources of media, such as Deadspin, have a proven track record in scrutinising and challenging power from outside the professional sport environment. After all, sports journalists work for news organisations that are emblematic of structural power and inequalities in society. However, sports journalists have access to resources and a professional obligation to public service. The question should therefore be whether these commitments are fulfilled in commercial and corporate news environments. Similarly, though, sports journalists must be careful not to use fifth-estate bloggers as a form of outsourcing that absolves them of their public-service duties. Other professional fields should be admitted in that they can bring depth and insight into issues, but this should not absolve sports journalists from acquiring the advanced knowledge and skills that are needed to report on such issues. Fifth-estate blogging has no concrete professional obligations to society, as such, and motivations can become problematic, particularly when we consider more questionable examples, such as Football Leaks and Fancy Bear.

The idea of sports journalists allowing their professional boundaries to be permeable becomes more problematic when we consider the different motivations of team media. Sports journalists must exert a degree of resistance against team media, which threaten to transform the notion of sports journalism into something else altogether. The fact that sports journalists regularly move into team media roles and accept their representation in public discussions on sports journalism is problematic. Here, advocacy for 'proper' and 'serious' journalism is likely to disappear from the conversation, with brand strategies and multimedia presentation coming to represent exemplars of 'good' sports journalism. For team media, this is partly motivated by a concerted strategy to gain greater credibility and legitimacy. Sports journalists who have become team media employees see sports journalism and team media as interchangeable, which means they perceive themselves as continued members of the occupational community (Mirer, 2019). It is rather ironic that at a time when legacy media are moving away from roles with the word 'journalist' in the title, the public relations industry is actively embracing it. Abbott (1988) identified publicity agents as the closest and biggest threat to journalism's jurisdiction and that point has never been truer for sports journalism than now. This blurring of boundaries is likely to continue apace as team media expands and legacy media contract (Hutchins & Boyle, 2017). In a professional context, sports journalists should recognise the inherent value of their missive and how these public service commitments are not interchangeable with the strategic aims of sports leagues and organisations. Sports journalism must therefore know when to protect its boundaries, such as in the case of team media, and when to allow the profession to accommodate other participants with genuine, altruistic aims to provide a public service and fifth-estate function, whether that be bloggers or athlete sports journalists.

Final thoughts

The future good health of professional sports journalism relies on three conditions. Firstly, sports journalists must demonstrate a professional commitment and desire to produce proper and serious stories. In doing so, sports journalists must develop a wide range of both official and unofficial sources and be prepared to collaborate with other actors for the public good. There needs to be less emphasis on commercial drivers, such as web metrics, and more focus on professional values. Serious sports journalism needs to be recognised as being the responsibility of every member of the professional group rather than niche positions within the newsroom. Further, entrants into the profession need to be motivated by making a difference rather than the opportunity to rub shoulders with their sporting heroes.

100 Conclusion

Secondly, news organisations must demonstrate an institutional commitment to producing serious and proper news journalism. The prevailing commercial attitude among sports desks is that worthy journalism does not sell and is simply produced for reputation and prestige. However, the mainstream media must recognise that it is the serious journalism that sets them apart from interlopers laying claim to their territory. Digital sports journalism is in the hands of news organisations who must decide whether to persist with its de-professionalisation or acknowledge that it requires greater critical and analytical skills going forward; again, to separate sports journalism from team media. It would certainly help on this front if The Athletic can prove itself to be profitable and sustainable, thus showing that proper sports journalism can also pay the bills.

Thirdly, sport clubs and leagues must allow sports journalists to be able to directly challenge and address those in power. The public will continue to expect transparency and openness. Recent developments, such as the aborted attempts by England's top six football clubs to join a breakaway European Super League, have shown that relations between sports owners and fans are currently at a low level. As football clubs attempt to repair that fractured relationship, they need to allow journalists to ask the challenging questions to go some way to restoring that public trust. The banning of reporters from press conferences and the increased restrictions on journalists during the COVID-19 pandemic is ultimately bad public relations that plays out unfavourably over social media.

Fifteen years ago, Boyle (2006) noted that there was a need for inquiring sports journalism in a sport environment that needed constant scrutiny. Things have only intensified in that direction, with Miller noting:

> corruption that is rife in ruling associations, the environmental impact of football, the role of podcasts in supporting the animal slavery and human addiction of gambling, and the systematic human-rights offences by team owners such as the heads of Paris Saint Germain, Girona and Manchester City.
>
> (Miller, 2021, p. 373)

Certainly, more so than in any other period, the digital age provides favourable conditions for sports journalists to banish their toy department reputation – the question is, can they put the ball in the net?

References

Abbott, A. (1988). *The System of Professions: An Essay on the Division of Expert Labour*. Chicago: University of Chicago Press.
Aldridge, M. (1998). The tentative hell-raisers: Identity and mythology in contemporary UK press journalism. *Media Culture & Society*, 20(1), 109–127. https://doi.org/10.1177/016344398020001007.
Aldridge, M. & Evetts, J. (2003). Rethinking the concept of professionalism: The case of journalism. *British Journal of Sociology*, 54(4), 547–564. https://doi.org/10.1111/j.1468-4446.2003.00547.x.
Allen, B. (2021, January 28). BetMGM inks partnership deal with The Athletic for sports betting. *Legal Sports Report*. Retrieved from https://www.legalsportsreport.com/47673/betmgm-partners-the-athletic/.
Allsop, J. (2020, July 28). The logistical and ethical challenges of sports reporters' restart. *Columbia Journalism Review*. Retrieved from https://www.cjr.org/the_media_today/sports_media_nba_bubble.php.
Anderson, C.W. (2008). Journalism: Expertise, authority, and power in democratic life. In D. Hesmondhalgh & J. Toynbee (Eds.), *The Media and Social Theory* (pp. 248–264). Abingdon: Routledge.
Anderson, C.W. & Schudson, M. (2008). Objectivity, professionalism and truth seeking in journalism. In K. Wahl-Jorgensen & T. Hanitzsch (Eds.), *The Handbook of Journalism Studies* (pp. 88–101). London: Routledge.
Antunovic, D. & Hardin, M. (2013). Women bloggers: Identity and the conceptualization of sports. *New Media & Society*, 15(8), 1374–1392. https://doi.org/10.1177/1461444812472323.
Associated Press (2019, October 22). AP to grow Major League Soccer coverage with automated stories. Retrieved from https://www.ap.org/press-releases/2019/ap-to-grow-major-league-soccer-coverage-with-automated-stories.
Awake, M. (2020, July 24). The comorbidities of the National Football League. *The New Yorker*. Retrieved from https://www.newyorker.com/culture/cultural-comment/the-comorbidities-of-the-national-football-league.
Bakowski, G., Goodwin, S. & Fisher, B. (2020, March 13). Premier League and British Football shuts down until April due to coronavirus – as it happened.

References

The Guardian. Retrieved from https://www.theguardian.com/football/live/2020/mar/13/premier-league-and-british-football-set-for-shutdown-due-to-coronavirus-live.

Bannerjee, R. (2020, October 15). Alex Kay-Jelski on how The Athletic persuaded a million readers to pay for sports journalism. *New Statesman*. Retrieved from https://www.newstatesman.com/politics/sport/2020/10/alex-kay-jelski-how-athletic-persuaded-million-readers-pay-sports-journalism.

Bauder, D. (2019, October 31). Order to 'stick to sports' has Deadspin site in open revolt. *Associated Press*. Retrieved from https://apnews.com/article/a22506e1e59d408f944f2b94c7d960f5.

Baxter, K. (2020, June 22). Introducing Kate Mason: Football Ramble's newest voice. *Stakhanov*. Retrieved from https://stakhanov.studio/articles/introducing-kate-mason-football-rambles-newest-voice/.

BBC (2010, April 7). That Mitchell and Webb Look: Football Rant. Retrieved from https://www.bbc.co.uk/programmes/p007803w.

BBC (2014, April 28). Bernie Ecclestone: Lies, Bribes and Formula One. Retrieved from https://www.bbc.co.uk/programmes/b042rbmg.

BBC (2017, February 20). David Walsh: Cycling's Team Sky boss 'duped me'. Retrieved from https://www.bbc.co.uk/news/av/uk-39032211.

BBC (2019a, September 18). Gareth Thomas: HIV and Me. Retrieved from https://www.bbc.co.uk/programmes/m0008yrh.

BBC (2019b, October 18). Spotlight on The Troubles: A secret history concludes with a series of revelations about the decades-long conflict. Retrieved from https://www.bbc.co.uk/mediacentre/latestnews/2019/spotlight-on-the-troubles.

BBC (2020a, October 29). BBC issues staff with new social media guidance. Retrieved from https://www.bbc.co.uk/news/entertainment-arts-54723282.

BBC (2020b, November 30). Anton Ferdinand: Football, Racism and Me. Retrieved from https://www.bbc.co.uk/programmes/m000pzpr.

BBC (2021, February 1). Boxing and the Mob. Retrieved from https://www.bbc.co.uk/programmes/m000ry0d.

BetMGM (2021, January 28). The Athletic and BetMGM announce exclusive sports betting partnership. *Cision*. Retrieved from https://www.prnewswire.com/news-releases/the-athletic-and-betmgm-announce-exclusive-sports-betting-partnership-301216988.html.

Birdsong, N. (2017, April 4). 4/4 NBA removes team-employed media from MVP voting. *Sporting News*. Retrieved from https://www.sportingnews.com/au/nba/news/nba-mvp-voting-results-harden-westbrook-team-employed-media-ban/1n7m85dycdv8l15wmemevfrzer.

Bossio, D. & Sacco, V. (2016). From 'selfies' to breaking tweets: How journalists negotiate personal and professional identity on social media. *Journalism Practice*, 11(5), 527–543. https://doi.org/10.1080/17512786.2016.1175314.

Boudway, I. (2019, August 20). The sports news site haters love to dunk on keeps signing up subscribers. *Bloomberg Businessweek*. Retrieved from https://www.bloomberg.com/news/features/2019-08-20/an-upstart-sports-news-service-is-thriving-amid-media-layoffs.

References 103

Bourdieu, P. (1993). *The Field of Cultural Production: Essays on Art and Literature*. New York: Columbia University Press.

Bourdieu, P. (2005). The political field, the social science field, and the journalistic field. In R. Benson & E. Neveu (Eds.), *Bourdieu and the Journalistic Field* (pp. 29–47). Cambridge: Polity Books.

Bournemouth Echo (2012). Cherries: Echo banned by football club. Retrieved from https://www.bournemouthecho.co.uk/sport/9601646.cherries-echo-banned-by-football-club/.

Boyle, R. (2006). *Sports Journalism: Context and Issues*. London: Sage.

Boyle, R. (2013). Reflections on communication and sport: On journalism and digital culture. *Communication & Sport*, 1(1/2), 88–99. https://doi.org/10.1177/2167479512467978.

Boyle, R. (2021). A new golden age? In R. Steen, J. Novick & H. Richards (Eds.), *Routledge Handbook of Sports Journalism* (pp. 355–358). Abingdon: Routledge.

Boyle, R. & Haynes, R. (2009). *Power Play: Sport, the Media and Popular Culture*. Edinburgh: Edinburgh University Press.

Boyle, R., Rowe, D. & Whannel, G. (2009). Delight in trivial controversy? Questions for sports journalism. In S. Allan (Ed.), *The Routledge Companion to News and Journalism* (pp. 245–255). London: Routledge.

Bradshaw, T. (2020). Sports journalism should toy with some different ideas. In J. Mair (Ed.), *The Virus and the Media: How British Journalists Covered the Pandemic* (pp. 92–96). Goring: Bite-Sized Books.

Bradshaw, T. & Minogue, D. (2019). *Sports Journalism: The State of Play*. Abingdon: Routledge.

Breen, M. (2020, July 27). After Covid-19 outbreak, the Marlins decided via group text message to play Sunday vs The Phillies. *Philadelphia Inquirer*. Retrieved from https://www.inquirer.com/phillies/miami-marlins-coronavirus-outbreak-phillies-mlb-season-20200727.html.

Bucholtz, A. (2020, June 5). The Athletic lays off 46 people, almost eight per cent of its staff. *Awful Announcing*. Retrieved from https://awfulannouncing.com/athletic/the-athletic-lays-off-46-people.html.

Bupp, P. (2020, November 5). The Athletic reportedly rescinds pandemic-related salary cuts for staff. *Awful Announcing*. Retrieved from https://awfulannouncing.com/athletic/the-athletic-reportedly-rescinds-pandemic-related-salary-cuts-for-staffers.html.

Burke, T. & Dickey, J. (2013, January 16). Manti Te'o's dead girlfriend, the most heartbreaking and inspirational story of the college football season, is a hoax. *Deadspin*. Retrieved from https://deadspin.com/manti-teos-dead-girlfriend-the-most-heartbreaking-an-5976517.

Burrell, I. (2019, July 21). How The Athletic is spending millions of pounds to shake up sports journalism. *iNews*. Retrieved from https://inews.co.uk/opinion/columnists/how-the-athletic-is-hoping-to-shake-up-the-world-of-sports-journalism-316563.

References

Burroughs, B. & Vogan, T. (2015). Media industries and sport scandals: Deadspin, *Sports Illustrated*, ESPN, and the Manti Te'o Hoax. *International Journal of Sport Communication*, 8(1), 87–102. https://doi.org/10.1123/IJSC.2014-0060.

Buschmann, R. & Wulzinger, M. (2018). *Football Leaks: Uncovering the Dirty Deals Behind the Beautiful Game*. London: Faber & Faber.

Buzzelli, N.R., Gentile, P., Billings, A.C. & Sadri, S.R. (2020). Poaching the news producers: The Athletic's effect on sports in hometown newspapers. *Journalism Studies*, 21(11), 1514–1530.

Buzzelli, N.R., Gentile, P., Sadri, S.R. & Billings, A.C. (2020). 'Cutting editors faster than we're cutting reporters': Influences of The Athletic on sports journalism quality and standards. *Communication & Sport*, 1–21. https://doi.org/10.1177/2167479520945658.

Cable, J. & Mottershead, G. (2018). 'Can I click it? Yes, you can': Football journalism, Twitter, and clickbait. *Ethical Space: The International Journal of Communication Ethics*, 15(1/2), 69–80.

Carlson, M. (2015). Introduction: The many boundaries of journalism. In M. Carlson & S. Lewis (Eds.), *Boundaries of Journalism: Professionalism, Practices and Participation* (pp. 1–18). Abingdon: Routledge.

Carlson, M. (2017). *Journalistic Authority: Legitimating News in the Digital Era*. New York: Columbia University Press.

Carlson, M. & Lewis, S. (Eds.) (2015). *Boundaries of Journalism: Professionalism, Practices and Participation*. Abingdon: Routledge.

Carr, C. (2020, July 17). Editor's note: How the Star Tribune is covering the Minnesota United at the MLS is Back tournament. *Minneapolis Star-Tribune*. Retrieved from https://www.startribune.com/editor-s-note-how-the-star-tribune-will-cover-the-minnesota-united-at-the-mls-is-back-tournament/571737142/.

Carragher, J. (2018). Exclusive: Jamie Carragher interviews Steven Gerrard – 'I've talked tactics with Rafa, but that's now impossible with Brendan Rodgers'. *The Telegraph*. Retrieved from https://www.telegraph.co.uk/football/2018/12/28/jamie-carragher-interviews-steven-gerrard-talked-tactics-rafa/.

Cash, R. (2020, April 8). What's a sports journalist to do when the coronavirus cancels all the games? As it turns out, plenty. *Poynter*. Retrieved from https://www.poynter.org/reporting-editing/2020/whats-a-sports-journalist-to-do-when-the-coronavirus-cancels-all-the-games-as-it-turns-out-plenty/.

Cassidy, W.P. (2017). Inching away from the toy department: Daily newspaper sports coverage of Jason Collins' and Michael Sam's coming out. *Communication & Sport*, 5(5), 534–553. https://doi.org/10.1177/2167479516642205.

Charlie Chaplin Big Fan (2020, February 13). Rosenthal on Astros' response to sign stealing, more. Accessed from https://www.youtube.com/watch?v=mYmR62_A5Fg.

Clavio, G. & Moritz, B. (2021). Here's why I joined: Introductory letters from new hires to The Athletic and the framing of paywall journalism. *Communication & Sport*, 9(2), 198–219. https://doi.org/10.1177/2167479519859862.

Conn, D. (2020, June 3). 'We were packed like sardines': Evidence grows of mass-event dangers early in the pandemic. *The Guardian*. Retrieved from

https://www.theguardian.com/world/2020/jun/03/we-were-packed-like-sardines-evidence-grows-of-mass-event-dangers-early-in-pandemic.
Conte, A. (2019, May 9). On media: How DK Pittsburgh Sports and The Athletic changed the game in sports coverage. *Next Pittsburgh*. Retrieved from https://nextpittsburgh.com/features/on-media-dkpittsburghsports-blazed-a-trail-the-athletic-and-others-are-continuing-the-disruption/.
Cosell, H. (1985). *I Never Played the Game*. New York: William Morrow & Company, Inc.
Curtis, B. (2019, May 29). 'The bane of my existence': UK sportswriting's access crisis. *The Ringer*. Retrieved from https://www.theringer.com/sports/2019/5/29/18643311/uk-sportswriting-embargo-access-champions-league-independent.
Curtis, B. (2020, July 15). Sports are coming back. Is sports media coming back with it? *The Ringer*. Retrieved from https://www.theringer.com/sports/2020/7/15/21325404/sports-return-coronavirus-nba-mlb-nfl-journalism-media.
Dart, J. (2009). Blogging the 2006 FIFA World Cup Finals. *Sociology of Sport Journal*, 26(1), 107–126. https://doi.org/10.1123/ssj.26.1.107.
Daum, E. & Scherer, J. (2018). Changing work routines and labour practices of sports journalists in the digital era: A case study of Postmedia. *Media, Culture & Society*, 40(4), 551–566. https://doi.org/10.1177/0163443717714992.
De Menezes, J. (2016, October 23). Victor Anichebe tweet leaves Sunderland striker red-faced after revealing his Twitter account isn't genuine. *The Independent*. Retrieved from https://www.independent.co.uk/sport/football/premier-league/victor-anichebe-tweet-deleted-twitter-account-sunderland-a7376536.html.
Deuze, M. (2005). What is journalism? Professional identity and ideology of journalists reconsidered. *Journalism*, 6(4), 442–464. https://doi.org/10.1177/1464884905056815.
Di Fino, N. (2021, January 28). What to expect from The Athletic's new sports betting section. *The Athletic*. Retrieved from https://theathletic.com/2350097/2021/01/28/what-to-expect-from-the-athletics-new-sports-betting-section/.
Di Stefano, M. (2019, July 17). 'It has set off a bomb': A US sports website has gone on a hiring spree of UK journalists. *BuzzFeed*. Retrieved from https://www.buzzfeed.com/markdistefano/athletic-hiring-spree.
Domeneghetti, R. (2017). *From the Back Page to the Front Room: Football's Journey Through the English Media* (2nd Ed). Huddersfield: Ockley Books.
Dowling, D. & Vogan, T. (2015). Can we snowfall this? Digital longform and the race for the tablet market. *Digital Journalism*, 3(2), 209–224. https://doi.org/10.1080/21670811.2014.930250.
Downie, A. (2018, April 18). Brazil's 'Let her do her job' campaign demands respect for female sports writers. *Committee to Protect Journalists*. Retrieved from https://cpj.org/2018/04/brazils-let-her-do-her-job-campaign-demands-respec/.
Doyel, G. (2020, July 21). In the coronavirus era, we're just dying to have sports. *Indianapolis Star*. Retrieved from https://eu.indystar.com/story/sports/2020/07/21/doyel-coronavirus-era-testing-shortages-were-dying-have-sports/5470664002/.

References

Draper, K. (2017, October 23). Why The Athletic wants to pillage newspapers. *New York Times*. Retrieved from https://www.nytimes.com/2017/10/23/sports/the-athletic-newspapers.html.

Draper, K. (2018, August 24). At The Athletic, a hiring spree becomes a story in itself. *New York Times*. Retrieved from https://www.nytimes.com/2018/08/24/sports/the-athletic-netflix.html.

Eldridge, S.A. (2018). 'Thank god for Deadspin': Interlopers, metajournalistic commentary, and fake news through the lens of 'journalistic realization'. *New Media & Society*, 2(4), 856–878. https://doi.org/10.1177/1461444818809461.

English, P. (2011). Online versus print: A comparative analysis of web-first sports coverage in Australia and the United Kingdom. *Media International Australia*, 140(1), 147–156. https://doi.org/10.1177/1329878X1114000118.

English, P. (2014). The same old stories: Exclusive news and uniformity of content in sports coverage. *International Journal of Sport Communication*, 7(4), 477–494. https://doi.org/10.1123/IJSC.2014-0026.

English, P. (2016). Mapping the sports journalism field: Bourdieu and broadsheet newsrooms. *Journalism*, 17(8), 1001–1017. https://doi.org/10.1177/1464884915576728.

Fischer, S. (2020a, January 21). Exclusive: The Athletic raises $50 million. *Axios*. Retrieved from https://www.axios.com/the-athletic-fundraising-round-series-de7026194-ccc7-4ec2-8415-6b8902c9a11a.html.

Fischer, S. (2020b, June 5). The Athletic lays off 8% of staff, implements company-wide pay cut. *Axios*. Retrieved from https://www.axios.com/the-athletic-layoffs-pay-cuts-fa15a80d-47b7-46a5-a08f-3e7eba558f30.html.

Forde, S. & Wilson, B. (2018). Radical sports journalism? Reflections on 'alternative' approaches to covering sport-related social issues. *Sociology of Sport Journal*, 35, 66–75. https://doi.org/10.1123/ssj.2017-0162.

Franklin-Wallis, O. (2020, March 2). Inside The Athletic: The start-up that changed journalism forever. *British GQ*. Retrieved from https://www.gq-magazine.co.uk/sport/article/the-athletic.

Galily, Y. (2018). Artificial intelligence and sports journalism? Is it a sweeping change? *Technology in Society*, 54, 47–51. https://doi.org/10.1016/j.techsoc.2018.03.001.

Gieryn, T. (1983). Boundary-work and the demarcation of science from non-science: Strains and interests in professional ideologies of scientists. *American Sociological Review*, 48(6), 781–795. https://doi.org/10.2307/2095325.

Glasspiegel, R. (2017, July 21). Can sportswriting online be saved? Vice Sports lays off writers, as the brutal year in sports media. *The Big Lead*. Retrieved from https://www.thebiglead.com/posts/can-sportswriting-online-be-saved-vice-sports-lays-off-writers-as-the-brutal-year-in-sports-media-01dm0xf8acfc.

Godfrey, H. (2020). From practice to piecemeal: Sports journalism in the Covid-19 era. *Ryerson University: Explanatory Journalism Project*. Retrieved from https://www.ryerson.ca/explanatory-journalism/spotlight-on-emerging-researchers/from-practice-to-piecemeal-sports-journalism-in-the-covid-19-era/.

References 107

Gold, A. (2021, March 15). Why Erik Lamela was yelling at the Tottenham bench and the two players Mourinho needs. *Football London*. Retrieved from https://www.football.london/tottenham-hotspur-fc/fixtures-results/lamela-doherty-bale-mourinho-arsenal-20155612.

Gray, J. (2020, September 18). After threatening its very existence, Covid-19 gave local sports reporting a whole new meaning. *journalism.co.uk*. Retrieved from https://www.journalism.co.uk/news/after-threatening-its-very-existence-covid-19-gave-local-sports-reporting-a-whole-new-meaning/s2/a761262/.

Hattenstone, S. (2018, August 23). All or nothing leaves City fans with more questions than answers. *The Guardian*. Retrieved from https://www.theguardian.com/football/blog/2018/aug/23/all-or-nothing-manchester-city-fans-documentary.

Heck, J. (2019, January 31). ESPN falls for fake LeBron James Instagram post about Anthony David trade rumors. *Sporting News*. Retrieved from https://www.sportingnews.com/us/nba/news/espn-falls-for-fake-lebron-james-instagram-post-about-anthony-davis-trade-rumors/m5kh8k5nf6m61d5mg2ug3yhkc.

Hermida, A. (2009). Blogging the BBC: Journalism blogs at 'the world's most trusted news organisation'. *Journalism Practice*, 3(3), 268–284. https://doi.org/10.1080/17512780902869082.

Higgerson, D. (2015, July 30). Why football writers shouldn't fear being banned by football clubs. Personal blog. Retrieved from https://davidhiggerson.wordpress.com/2015/07/30/why-football-writers-shouldnt-fear-being-banned-by-football-clubs/#more-6310.

Houghton, A. (2019, August 29). Meet the journalist: The Athletic's Alex-Kay Jelski. *Cision*. Retrieved from https://www.cision.co.uk/category/industry-news/meet-the-journalist-the-athletic-uk-alex-kay-jelski/.

Hunter, R. (2020, September 24). Despite its best intentions, football remains unwelcoming of gay fans. *The Guardian*. Retrieved from https://www.theguardian.com/football/2020/sep/24/despite-its-best-intentions-football-remains-unwelcoming-of-gay-fans.

Hutchins, B. & Boyle, R. (2017). A community of practice: Sport journalism, mobile media and institutional change. *Digital Journalism*, 5(5), 496–512. https://doi.org/10.1080/21670811.2016.1234147.

Hutchins, B. & Mikosza, J. (2010). The Web 2.0 Olympics: Athlete blogging, social networking and policy contradictions at the 2008 Beijing Games. *Convergence*, 16(3), 279–297. https://doi.org/10.1177/1354856510367618.

Hutchins, B. & Rowe, D. (2009). From broadcast scarcity to digital plenitude: The changing dynamics of the media sport content economy. *Television & New Media*, 10(4), 354–370. https://doi.org/10.1177/1527476409334016.

Hutchins, B. & Rowe, D. (2012). *Sport Beyond Television: The Internet, Digital Media and the Rise of Networked Sport*. London: Routledge.

Ingle, S. (2016, September 15). What is a TUE? 11 key questions on the Fancy Bears WADA leaks. *The Guardian*. Retrieved from https://www.theguardian.com/sport/2016/sep/15/tue-fancy-bears-wada-leaks.

Ingle, S. (2020, December 30). Leeds United condemn abuse of Karen Carney after club tweet mocked pundit. *The Guardian*. Retrieved from https://www.

theguardian.com/football/2020/dec/30/leeds-united-criticised-for-tweet-mocking-amazon-pundit-karen-carney.
James, L. (2020, February 3). How The Athletic is disrupting sports journalism. *The Boar*. Retrieved from https://theboar.org/2020/02/how-the-athletic-disrupting-sports-journalism/.
Johnson, M. (2018, January 25). Johnson column: The good ol' cricket press box is just not the same as it once was. *The Cricket Paper*. Retrieved from https://thecricketpaper.com/featured/4035/johnson-column-the-good-ol-cricket-press-box-is-just-not-the-same-as-it-once-was/.
Joseph, S. (2020, March 11). How football clubs are becoming more like media business. *Digiday*. Retrieved from https://digiday.com/marketing/football-clubs-becoming-like-media-businesses/.
Kalaf, S. (2017, August 8). Fox Sports is having a little trouble with that pivot. *Deadspin*. Retrieved from https://deadspin.com/fox-sports-is-having-a-little-trouble-with-that-pivot-1797651478.
Kelly, C. (2020, June 28). We had a good run, but things are about to get weird for sports journalists. *The Globe and Mail*. Retrieved from https://www.theglobeandmail.com/sports/article-we-had-a-good-run-but-things-are-about-to-get-weird-for-sports/.
Keown, M. (2020, May 29). 'I didn't have to look for the ball at my feet … I could do that blindfolded': Martin Keown catches up with fellow Arsenal legend Dennis Berkamp about his fear of flying, practical jokes and THAT Newcastle goal. *Mail Online*. Retrieved from https://www.dailymail.co.uk/sport/football/article-8370137/Martin-Keown-catches-fellow-Arsenal-legend-Dennis-Bergkamp-Newcastle-goal.html.
Kian, E., Burden, Jr, J.W. & Shaw, S. (2011). Internet sport bloggers: Who are these people and where do they come from? *Journal of Sport Administration and Supervision*, 3(1), 30–43.
Kimmage, P. (2016, September 25). Paul Kimmage: So many questions not asked, so many questions remain unanswered. *Sunday Independent*. Retrieved from https://www.independent.ie/sport/other-sports/paul-kimmage-so-many-questions-not-asked-so-many-questions-remain-unanswered-35076219.html.
Kludt, T. (2020, July 21). 'You don't want to be the domino': Reporters inside the NBA's Covid-free bubble are hoping it doesn't burst. *Vanity Fair*. Retrieved from https://www.vanityfair.com/news/2020/07/inside-the-nbas-covid-free-bubble.
Kroon, A. & Eriksson, G. (2019). The impact of the digital transformation on sports journalism talk online. *Journalism Practice*, 13(7), 834–852. https://doi.org/10.1080/17512786.2019.1577695.
Kunert, J. (2020). Automation in sports reporting: Strategies of data providers, software providers, and media outlets. *Media and Communication*, 8(3), 5–15. http://dx.doi.org/10.17645/mac.v8i3.2996.
Kuty, B. (2020, July 4). Yankees' Masahiro Tanaka hit in head by Giancarlo Stanton line drive. *NJ.com*. Retrieved from https://www.nj.com/yankees/2020/07/yankees-masahiro-tanaka-hurt-hit-line-drive-from-giancarlo-stanton.html.

References

Lange, K.M., Nicholson, M. & Hess, R. (2007). A new breed apart? Work practices of Australian internet sport journalists. *Sport in Society*, 10(4), 662–679.

Larson, M.S. (1977). *The Rise of Professionalism: A Sociological Analysis*. Berkeley: University of California Press.

Leitch, W. (2009, November 10). 'Bill Simmons, Establishment'. *Deadspin*. Retrieved from https://deadspin.com/bill-simmons-establishment-5401300.

Lewis, S. (2012). The tension between professional control and open participation: Journalism and its boundaries. *Information, Communication & Society*, 15(6), 836–866. https://doi.org/10.1080/1369118X.2012.674150.

Liew, J. (2020, October 3). A mural in time: Imagining Shane Warne's ultimate party. *The Guardian*. Retrieved from https://www.theguardian.com/sport/2020/oct/04/a-mural-in-time-imagining-shane-warnes-ultimate-party.

Local Media Consortium (2020, July 27). Local Media Consortium to launch The Matchup with deep coverage on professional and college sports. *Local Media Consortium*. Retrieved from https://www.localmediaconsortium.com/post/local-media-consortium-to-launch-the-matchup-with-deep-coverage-on-professional-and-college-sports.

Lowes, M.D. (1999). *Inside the Sports Pages: Work Routines, Professional Ideologies and the Manufacture of Sports News*. Toronto: University of Toronto Press.

Lowes, M. & Robillard, C. (2018). Social media and digital breakage on the sports beat. *International Journal of Sport Communication*, 11(3), 308–318. https://doi.org/10.1123/ijsc.2018-0088.

Manfred, T. (2015, May 14). Why Bill Simmons was fired. *Business Insider*. Retrieved from https://www.businessinsider.com/why-bill-simmons-got-fired-2015-5?r=US&IR=T.

Mayhew, F. (2020a, April 7). News publishers hit new online records with coronavirus coverage. *Press Gazette*. Retrieved from https://www.pressgazette.co.uk/ft-and-reach-titles-hit-new-online-records-with-coronavirus-coverage/.

Mayhew, F. (2020b, April 28). Sports journalists share fears Covid-19 cuts could be permanent as industry weakened. *Press Gazette*. Retrieved from https://www.pressgazette.co.uk/sports-journalists-share-fears-covid-19-cuts-could-be-permanent-as-industry-weakened/.

McCarthy, B. (2013). Consuming sports media, producing sports media: An analysis of two fan sports blogospheres. *International Review for the Sociology of Sport*, 48(4), 421–434. https://doi.org/10.1177/1012690212448240.

McCarthy, B. (2014). A sports journalism of their own: An investigation into the motivations, behaviours, and media attitudes of fan sports bloggers. *Communication & Sport*, 2(1), 65–79. https://doi.org/10.1177/2167479512469943.

McCaskill, S. (2019, January 21). Sport is on the brink of a digital revolution. *Forbes*. Retrieved from https://www.forbes.com/sites/stevemccaskill/2019/01/21/sport-is-on-the-brink-of-a-digital-revolution-in-2019/#6329acef24b7.

McEnnis, S. (2013). Raising our game: Effects of citizen journalism on Twitter for professional identity and working practices of British sports journalists. *International Journal of Sport Communication*, 6(4), 423–433. https://doi.org/10.1123/ijsc.6.4.423.

McEnnis, S. (2016). Following the action: How live bloggers are reimagining the professional ideology of sports journalism. *Journalism Practice*, 10(8), 967–982. https://doi.org/10.1080/17512786.2015.1068130.

McEnnis, S. (2017). Playing on the same pitch: Attitudes of sports journalists towards fan bloggers. *Digital Journalism*, 5(5), 549–566. https://doi.org/10.1080/21670811.2016.1246374.

McEnnis, S. (2018a). A comparative analysis of how regulatory codes inform broadcast and print sports journalists' work routines in the UK using Sky Sports News and The Sun as case studies. *Ethical Space: The International Journal of Communication Ethics*, 15(1–2), 43–51.

McEnnis, S. (2018b). Sports journalism and cultural authority in the digital age. In D. Burdsey, T. Carter & M. Doidge (Eds.), *Transforming Sport: Knowledges, Practices and Structures* (pp. 207–219). Abingdon: Routledge.

McEnnis, S. (2020). Toy department within the toy department? Online sports journalists and professional legitimacy. *Journalism*, 21(10), 1415–1431. https://doi.org/10.1177/1464884918797613.

McEnnis, S. (2021a). Sports journalism and Twitter. In R. Steen, J. Novick & H. Edwards (Eds.), *Routledge Handbook of Sports Journalism* (pp. 125–134). Abingdon: Routledge.

McEnnis, S. (2021b). (Un)bunch of amateurs: Locating the fifth estate in the sports blogosphere. In R. Domeneghetti (Ed.), *Reporting Sports in the Digital Age: Theoretical and Ethical Considerations in a Changing Media Landscape* (pp. 49–62). Abingdon: Routledge.

McGran, K. (2020, July 23). NHL is using coronavirus to choke off media access. *Toronto Star*. Retrieved from https://www.thestar.com/sports/breakawa y_blog/2020/07/23/nhl-is-using-coronavirus-to-choke-off-media-access.html.

McGuire, J. & Murray, R. (2014). Attitudes of sport print journalists about developing electronic media skills: A case study of two major newspapers. *International Journal of Sport Communication*, 6(4), 464–477. https://doi.org/10.1177/0739532916634648.

McGuire, J. & Murray, R. (2016). New work demands create inequity for sports journalists. *Newspaper Research Journal*, 37(1), 58–69. https://doi.org/10.1177/0739532916634648.

McKenzie, J. & Fisher, L. (2017, October 5). Female sports journalist react to Cam Newton, share their own sexist experiences. *ABC News*. Retrieved from https://a bcnews.go.com/Entertainment/female-sports-journalists-react-cam-newton-share-sexist/story?id=50304858.

McMullan, C. (2017, September 28). Man City and Chelsea Instagram gaffe reveals hypocritical nature of football news. *Digital Sport*. Retrieved from https://digitalsport.co/man-city-and-chelsea-instagram-gaffe-reveals-hypocri tical-nature-of-football-news.

Meltzer, K. (2009). The hierarchy of journalistic cultural authority: Journalists' perspectives according to news medium. *Journalism Practice*, 3(1) 59–74. https://doi.org/10.1080/17512780802560757.

Miller, T. (2021) Reporting. In R. Steen, J. Novick & H. Richards (Eds.), *Routledge Handbook of Sports Journalism* (pp. 367–376). Abingdon: Routledge.

Mirer, M. (2019). Playing the right way: In-house sports reporters and media ethics as boundary work. *Journal of Media Ethics*, 34(2), 73–86. https://doi.org/10.1080/23736992.2019.1599719.

Moritz, B. (2015). The story versus the stream: Digital media's influence on newspaper sports journalism. *International Journal of Sport Communication*, 8, 397–410. https://doi.org/10.1123/ijsc.2015-0071.

Moritz, B. (2020, December). The year sports journalism changes for good. *Nieman Lab*. Retrieved from https://www.niemanlab.org/2020/12/the-year-sports-journalism-changes-for-good/.

Morrison, S. (2014, July/August). The toy department shall lead us: Why sports media have always been newsroom innovators. *Columbia Journalism Review*. Retrieved from https://archives.cjr.org/reports/the_toy_department_shall_lead.php.

Mullin, B. (2020, July 26). As the NBA restarts, fewer reporters get sent to cover it. *The Wall Street Journal*. Retrieved from https://www.wsj.com/articles/as-the-nba-restarts-fewer-reporters-get-sent-to-cover-it-11595779601.

Naylor, A. (2019, September 23). 'When has he ever done that?' – watching Burn's Newcastle return with his schoolmates. *The Athletic*. Retrieved from https://theathletic.com/1229982/2019/09/23/when-has-he-ever-done-that-watching-burns-newcastle-return-with-his-schoolmates/.

Nicholls, A. (2019, October 19). The dilemma of the poacher turned gamekeeper. *CIPR Education Skills Sector*. Retrieved from https://cipredskills.com/uncategorized/the-dilemma-of-the-poacher-turned-gamekeeper/.

Nilsson, P. (2020, March 24). The Athletic suffers identity crisis over cancelled sports fixtures. *Financial Times*. Retrieved from https://www.ft.com/content/48cb7940-69dc-11ea-800d-da70cff6e4d3.

Oates, T.P. & Pauly, J. (2007). Sports journalism as moral and ethical discourse. *Journal of Mass Media Ethics*, 22(4), 332–347. https://doi.org/10.1080/08900520701583628.

O'Brien, S. (2019, May 20). Bad timing? Danny Murphy clashes with journalist who asked Pep Guardiola about Financial Fair Play after FA Cup triumph. *talkSPORT*. Retrieved from https://talksport.com/football/fa-cup/545903/danny-murphy-pep-guardiola-financial-fair-play-fa-cup/.

O'Donnell, J. (2019, May 20). 'They think we should deny the public context' – Rob Harris on Manchester City. *OTB Sports*. Retrieved from https://www.otbsports.com/soccer/think-deny-public-context-rob-harris-manchester-city-861122.

Ornebring, H. (2009). The two professionalisms of journalism: Journalism and the changing context of work. *Reuters Institute for the Study of Journalism*. Retrieved from https://reutersinstitute.politics.ox.ac.uk/sites/default/files/2017-11/The%20Two%20Professionalisms%20of%20Journalism_Working%20Paper.pdf.

Pellatt, C. (2020, October 16). I was blocked from asking Harry Kane about Black Lives Matter – we need to know why. *Versus*. Retrieved from https://versus.uk.com/2020/10/i-blocked-asking-harry-kane-black-lives-matter-need-know/.

Pickard, V. & Williams, A.T. (2014). Salvation or folly? The promises and perils of digital paywalls. *Digital Journalism*, 2(2), 195–213. https://doi.org/10.1080/21670811.2013.865967.
Politi, S. (2020, July 6). Sports are back (for now). Sportswriters? We're still on the sidelines. *NJ.com*. Retrieved from https://www.nj.com/yankees/2020/07/sports-are-back-sportswriters-were-still-on-the-sidelines-politi.html.
Praverman, F. (2010, March 24). Mike Atherton named Sports Journalist of the Year at British Press Awards. *The Times*. Retrieved from https://www.thetimes.co.uk/article/mike-atherton-named-sports-journalist-of-the-year-at-british-press-awards-6c8jc27p0rj.
Press Gazette (2011, September 5). Scottish football blogger faces 'ban' after breaking post-match comments. Retrieved from https://www.pressgazette.co.uk/scottish-football-blogger-faces-ban-after-breaking-post-match-comments-embargo/.
Ramon, X. & Tulloch, C.D. (2019). Life beyond clickbait journalism: A transnational study of the independent football magazine market. *Communication & Sport*, 1–22. https://doi.org/10.1177/2167479519878674.
Rathborn, J. (2020, December 31). Manchester United's Edinson Cavani banned for three games over Instagram post. *The Independent*. Retrieved from https://www.independent.co.uk/sport/football/premier-league/manchester-united/edinson-cavani-ban-instagram-fa-b1780904.html.
Redford, P. (2017, October 23). What is The Athletic's plan beyond exterminating newspapers? *Deadspin*. Retrieved from https://deadspin.com/what-is-the-athletics-plan-beyond-exterminating-newspap-1819776358.
Reed, S. & Harrison, G. (2019). Insider dope and NBA trade coverage: A case study of unnamed sourcing in sports journalism. *International Journal of Sport Communication*, 12(3), 419–430. https://doi.org/10.1123/ijsc.2019-0012.
Reynolds. J. (2019, August 3). US upstart The Athletic sends shockwaves through British football media. *The Irish Times*. Retrieved from https://www.irishtimes.com/sport/soccer/english-soccer/us-upstart-the-athletic-sends-shockwaves-through-british-football-media-1.3974420.
Richards, A. (2018, June 13). Spanish reporter uses Google translate after French player Antoine Griezmann refuses to answer transfer questions in a foreign language. *Evening Standard*. Retrieved from https://www.standard.co.uk/news/world/spanish-reporter-uses-google-translate-after-french-footballer-refuses-to-answer-questions-in-any-other-language-to-avoid-being-asked-about-transfer-rumours-a3862061.html.
Robson, L. (2019, August 14). How new sport website the Athletic is disrupting Fleet Street. *New Statesman*. Retrieved from https://www.newstatesman.com/politics/sport/2019/08/how-new-sport-website-athletic-disrupting-fleet-street.
Rojas-Torrijos, J. (2019). Automated sports coverage. Case study of bot released by *The Washington Post* during the Rio 2016 and PyeongChang 2018 Olympics. *Revista Latina de Communicacion Social*, 1729–1747. https://doi.org/10.4185/RLCS-2019-1407.

References

Rojas-Torrijos, J. (2020). Gamification of sports media coverage: An infotainment approach to Olympics and Football World Cups. *Communication & Society*, 33(1), 29–44. https://doi.org/10.15581/003.33.1.29-44.

Rojas-Torrijos, J. & Toural Bran, C. (2019). Automated sports journalism: The AnaFut case study, the bot developed by El Confidencial for writing football match reports. *Doxa Communicacion*, 29, 235–254. https://doi.org/10.31921/doxacom.n29a12.

Rosenthal, K. & Drellich, E. (2019, November 12). The Astros stole signs electronically in 2017 – part of a much broader issue for Major League Baseball. *The Athletic*. Retrieved from https://theathletic.co.uk/1363451/2019/11/12/the-astros-stole-signs-electronically-in-2017-part-of-a-much-broader-issue-for-major-league-baseball/.

Rowe, D. (2004). *Sport, Media and Culture: The Unruly Trinity* (2nd Ed). Oxford: Oxford University Press.

Rowe, D. (2007). Sports journalism: Still the 'toy department' of the news media? *Journalism*, 8(4), 385–405. https://doi.org/10.1177/1464884907078657.

Rowe, D. (2017). Sports journalism and the FIFA scandal: Personalization, co-optation and investigation. *Communication & Sport*, 5(5), 515–533. https://doi.org/10.1177/2167479516642206.

Rowe, S. (2015, October). Media training and the art of saying nothing. *FourFourTwo Magazine*. Bath: Future plc.

Salwen, M. & Garrison, B. (1998). Finding their place in journalism: Newspaper sports' journalists' professional 'problems'. *Journal of Sport & Social Issues*, 22(1), 88–102. https://doi.org/10.1177/019372398022001008.

Sandomir, R. & Miller, J. (2013, January 22). As ESPN debated, Manti Te'o story slipped away. *New York Times*. https://www.nytimes.com/2013/01/23/sports/ncaafootball/as-debate-raged-at-espn-manti-teo-story-slipped-from-its-hands.html.

Schmidt, C. (2017, July 25). The Athletic, that local sports startup with no advertising, raises $5.4million and scoops up *Sports Illustrated*'s former top editor. *Nieman Lab*. Retrieved from https://www.niemanlab.org/2017/07/the-athletic-that-local-sports-startup-with-no-advertising-raises-5-4-million-and-scoops-up-sports-illustrateds-former-top-editor/.

Schwartz, D. & Vogan, T. (2017). The Players' Tribune: Self-branding and boundary work in digital sports media. *Journal of Sports Media*, 12(1), 45–63. https://doi.org/10.1353/jsm.2017.0002.

Serazio, M. (2021). The irreverent life and uncompromising death of Deadspin: Sports blogging as punk journalism. *Journalism*, 1–18. https://doi.org/10.1177/1464884920987690.

Sharman, D. (2018, December 19). Ex-editor brands regional news site 'idiots' for covering Mourinho sacking. *Hold the Front Page*. Retrieved from https://www.holdthefrontpage.co.uk/2018/news/ex-editor-brands-regional-news-site-idiots-for-covering-mourinho-sacking/?utm_source=dlvr.it&utm_medium=twitter.

Sharman, D. (2020, November 13). Readers' toxic behaviour has sparked crisis for sports journalists, content boss says. *Hold the Front Page.* Retrieved from https://www.holdthefrontpage.co.uk/2020/news/readers-toxic-behaviour-has-led-to-crisis-for-sports-journalists-content-boss-says/.

Sharman, D. (2021, February 11). Football boss hits out at club-controlled journalism. *Hold the Front Page.* Retrieved from https://www.holdthefrontpage.co.uk/2021/news/football-manager-compares-club-controlled-journalism-to-communist-state/.

Sheffer, M.L. & Schultz, B. (2010). Paradigm shift or passing fad? Twitter and sports journalism. *International Journal of Sport Communication,* 3(4), 472–484. https://doi.org/10.1123/ijsc.3.4.472.

Sherman, A. (2020, September 9). The Athletic says it hits 1 million subscribers after surviving sports shutdown. *CNBC.* Retrieved from https://www.cnbc.com/2020/09/09/the-athletic-hits-1-million-subscribers-after-enduring-sports-shutdown.html.

Sherwood, M. & Nicholson, M. (2013). Web 2.0 platforms and the work of newspaper sport journalists. *Journalism,* 14(7), 942–959. https://doi.org/10.1177/1464884912458662.

Sherwood, M., Nicholson, M. & Marjoribanks, T. (2017a). Access, agenda building and information subsidies: Media relations in professional sport. *International Review for the Sociology of Sport,* 52(8), 992–1007. https://doi.org/10.1177/1012690216637631.

Sherwood, M., Nicholson, M. & Marjoribanks, T. (2017b). Controlling the message and the medium? The impact of sports organisations' digital and social channels on media access. *Digital Journalism,* 5(5), 513–531. https://doi.org/10.1080/21670811.2016.1239546.

Sims, D. (2015, October 30). Goodnight and thank you, Grantland. *The Atlantic.* Retrieved from https://www.theatlantic.com/entertainment/archive/2015/10/rip-grantland/413443/.

Singer, J. (2005). The political j-blogger: 'Normalizing' a new media form to fit old norms and practices. *Journalism,* 6(2), 173–198. https://doi.org/10.1177/1464884905051009.

Sky Sports (2021a, March 16). Sky Sports unites against online hate and abuse: 'It has to stop'. Retrieved from https://www.skysports.com/more-sports/news/11095/12086666/sky-sports-unites-against-online-hate-and-abuse-it-has-to-stop.

Sky Sports (2021b, May 12). Joe Marler discusses battle with depression and goes on journey to rebuild his mental health in Sky Sports' Big Boys Don't Cry. Retrieved from https://www.skysports.com/rugby-union/news/12321/12303342/joe-marler-discusses-battle-with-depression-and-goes-on-journey-to-rebuild-his-mental-health-in-sky-sports-big-boys-dont-cry.

Smith, A.B. & Whiteside, E. (2021). From taped up to mic'd up: Experiences of former athletes and the meaning of athletic identity in sports media spaces. *Communication & Sport,* 9(2), 220–242. https://doi.org/10.1177/2167479519858611.

References

Sports Journalists' Association (SJA) (2020a, August 18). The Athletic recruit Telegraph's Katie Whyatt as women's football correspondent. Retrieved from https://www.sportsjournalists.co.uk/journalism-news/the-athletic-recruit-telegraphs-katie-whyatt-as-womens-football-correspondent/.

Sports Journalists' Association (SJA) (2020b, November 12). SJA Notebook: Toxic culture exposed, accreditation woes and popular Vera retires. Retrieved from https://www.sportsjournalists.co.uk/journalism-news/sja-notebook-toxic-culture-exposed-accreditation-woes-and-popular-vera-retires/.

Sports Journalists' Association (SJA) (2021, March 15). The 2020 SJA British Journalism Awards winners. Retrieved from https://www.sportsjournalists.co.uk/awards-news/the-2020-sja-british-sports-journalism-awards-winners/.

Steen, R. (2007). *Sports Journalism: A Multimedia Primer*. London: Routledge.

Strauss, B. (2020, March 4). Sportswriting's future may depend on The Athletic, which is either re-assuring or terrifying. *The Washington Post*. Retrieved from https://www.washingtonpost.com/sports/2020/03/03/the-athletic-sports-media-future/.

Sugden, J. & Tomlinson, A. (2007). Stories from Planet Football and Sportsworld: Source relations and collusion in sports journalism. *Journalism Practice*, 1(1), 44–61. https://doi.org/10.1080/17512780601078860.

Sugden, J. & Tomlinson, A. (2010). What Beckham had for breakfast: The rolling menu of 24/7 sports news. In J. Lewis & S. Cushion (Eds.), *The Rise of 24-hour News Television: Global Perspectives* (pp. 151–166). Oxford: Peter Lang.

Suggs Jr, D.W. (2015). Valuing the media: Access and autonomy as functions of legitimacy for journalists. *International Journal of Sport Communication*, 8(1), 46–67. https://doi.org/10.1123/IJSC.2014-0074.

Suggs Jr, D.W. (2016). Tensions in the press box: Understanding relationships among sports media and source organizations. *Communication & Sport*, 4 (3), 261–281. https://doi.org/10.1177/2167479515577191.

Sutton, C. (2019, November 15). Ronaldinho called him 'idolo', Sir Alex Ferguson says he is a 'football aristocrat' and at Celtic, he is 'The King of Kings' ... Henrik Larsson reflects on his career with Chris Sutton, his old partner in crime. *Mail Online*. Retrieved from https://www.dailymail.co.uk/sport/football/article-7690775/Chris-Sutton-travels-Sweden-meet-old-partner-crime-Henrik-Larsson-talk-Celtic.html.

Syed, M. (2016, January 25). Football Leaks in fear for trying to make the game more transparent. *The Times*. Retrieved from https://www.thetimes.co.uk/article/syed-football-leaks-in-fear-for-trying-to-make-game-transparent-ff23xdzvh.

Tameez, H. (2020, March 16). What do sports journalists do when there are no sports to cover? *Nieman Lab*. Retrieved from https://www.niemanlab.org/2020/03/what-do-sports-journalists-do-when-there-are-no-sports-to-cover/.

The Guardian (2012, February 29). Sean Ingle on open sport journalism: 'If we weren't open we would be behind our rivals'. Retrieved from https://www.theguardian.com/media/video/2012/feb/29/sean-ingle-open-sport-journalism-video.

References

Thurman, N. (2008). Forums for citizen journalists? Adoption of user generated content initiatives by online news media. *New Media & Society*, 10(1), 139–157. https://doi.org/10.1177/1461444807085325.

Thurman, N. & Walters, A. (2013). Live blogging – digital journalism's pivotal platform? A case study of the production, consumption and form of live blogs at guardian.co.uk. *Digital Journalism*, 1(1), 82–101. https://doi.org/10.1080/21670811.2012.714935.

Tomlinson, A. (2016). Twitter and the rolling–news agenda on sports channels. In S. Cushion & R. Sambrook (Eds.), *The Future of 24-hour News: New Directions, New Challenges* (pp. 213–226). New York: Peter Lang.

Toonkel, J. & Dolan, T. (2020, June 3). The Athletic and Bleacher Report consider betting deals. *The Information*. Retrieved from https://www.theinformation.com/articles/the-athletic-and-bleacher-report-consider-betting-deals.

Turberville, H. (2018, March 23). Mike Atherton at 50: A lightning rise from England captain to four-time cricket correspondent of the year. *The Cricketer*. Retrieved from https://www.thecricketer.com/Topics/special2/mike_atherton_at_50_a_lightning_rise_from_england_captain_to_four-time_cricket_correspondent_of_the_year.html.

Vanek Smith, S. (2018, March 5). How 'Icarus' accidentally exposed a major 'Oceans Eleven-style' doping scheme. *NPR*. Retrieved from https://www.npr.org/2018/03/05/590869276/how-icarus-accidentally-exposed-a-major-ocean-s-eleven-style-doping-scheme.

Varley, C. (2020, September 7). All or Nothing: Jose Mourinho's soft side, and Danny Rose wants answers. *BBC Sport*. Retrieved from https://www.bbc.co.uk/sport/football/54062068.amp.

Vimieiro, A.C. (2018). The digital productivity of football supporters: Formats, motivations and styles. *Convergence*, 24(4), 374–390. https://doi.org/10.1177/1354856516678396.

Vogan, T. (2012). ESPN Films and the construction of prestige in contemporary sports television. *International Journal of Sport Communication*, 5(2), 137–152. https://doi.org/10.1123/ijsc.5.2.137.

Vogan, T. & Dowling, D. (2016). Bill Simmons, Grantland.com, and ESPN's corporate reinvention of literary sports writing online. *Convergence*, 22(1), 18–34. https://doi.org/10.1177/1354856514550637.

Wagner, L. (2018, August 23). The Athletic fails to raid the *Washington Post* sports desk. *Deadspin*. Retrieved from https://deadspin.com/the-athletic-fails-to-raid-the-washington-post-sports-d-1828532944.

Wahl-Jorgensen, K. (2016). Emotion and journalism. In T. Witschge, C.W. Anderson, D. Domingo & A. Hermida (Eds.), *The SAGE Handbook of Digital Journalism* (pp. 128–143). London: Sage.

Waisbord, S. (2013). *Reinventing Professionalism: Journalism and News in Global Perspective*. Cambridge: Polity.

Wall, M. (2019). *Citizen Journalism: Practices, Propaganda, Pedagogy*. Abingdon: Routledge.

References

Wallace, J. (2020, October 8). The class ceiling: Does the England cricket team suffer for its elitism. *The Guardian*. Retrieved from https://www.theguardian.com/sport/2020/oct/08/the-class-ceiling-does-england-cricket-team-suffer-elitism.

Walsh, J.D. (2019, November 9). The senseless death of Deadspin. *New York Magazine*. Retrieved from https://nymag.com/intelligencer/2019/11/deadspins-senseless-death.html.

Warner, J. (2016, May 11). The Biblioracle: Remembering George Plimpton's sports books. *Chicago Tribune*. Retrieved from https://www.chicagotribune.com/entertainment/books/ct-prj-biblioracle-george-plimpton-20160511-column.html.

Waterson, J. (2019, January 24). BuzzFeed to lay off 200 staff in latest round of cuts. *The Guardian*. Retrieved from https://www.theguardian.com/media/2019/jan/24/buzzfeed-to-lay-off-200-staff-in-latest-round-of-cuts.

Weedon, G., Wilson, B., Yoon, L. & Lawson, S. (2016). Where's all the 'good' sports journalism? Sports media research, the sociology of sport, and the question of quality sports reporting. *International Review for the Sociology of Sport*, 53(6), 639–667.

Wenner, L. (2011). Mocking the fan for profit: Sports dirt, fanship identity and commercial narratives. In A. Billings (Ed.), *Sports Media: Transformation, Integration, Consumption* (pp. 61–77). New York: Routledge.

Wright, I. (2021). Ian Wright: Home Truths – 'a lot of my anger was pain and unhappiness'. *BBC*. Retrieved from https://www.bbc.co.uk/sport/football/57000650.

Yoder, M. (2013, January 24). How Deadspin beat ESPN to the Manti Te'o scoop. *Awful Announcing*. Retrieved from https://awfulannouncing.com/2013/how-deadspin-beat-espn-to-the-manti-te-o-scoop.html.

Zelizer, B. (1992). *Covering the Body: The Kennedy Assassination, the Media and the Shaping of Collective Memory*. Chicago: University of Chicago Press.

Zornosa, L. (2020, July 7). Megan Rapinoe enlists Alexandria Ocasio-Cortez for HBO series on social change. *Los Angeles Times*. Retrieved from https://www.latimes.com/entertainment-arts/tv/story/2020-07-27/megan-rapinoe-alexandria-ocasio-cortez-hbo-sports.

Index

24-hour rolling news 15, 42, 58, 60, 66

Abbott, A. 6, 54–5, 99
access: changing boundaries 44–7; exclusive: sports journalists in empty stadiums 87–9; future of 96–7; insider 3–4, 17–18, 46, 77, 88, 98; restrictions 3, 15, 55, 89
accreditation: The Athletic 79; background 3; digital sports journalism 20, 23; the future 96; sports blogging 28–9, 33–4, 36–7, 40; sports public relations 43, 45, 53–6
Aldridge, M. 8
Allen, Justin 36
Allsop, J. 89
Amazon 46, 51, 74
America *see* US
Anderson, C.W. 2
Antunovic, D. 32
Associated Press 23, 25, 53, 84
athlete sports journalism 57–68; background 57–8; conclusions 66–8; future considerations 99; print versus broadcast sports journalism 58–61; rise of athlete sports journalism 61–6; sports journalists and the professional crisis 10
Athletic, The 69–81; conclusions 79–81; COVID-19 and sports journalism 89–91; disruptive business model 69–72; future considerations 95, 100; making it work 72–6; and professional practice 76–9; subscription-based models 10–11
Australia 16, 23, 39, 44, 48, 82

BBC (British Broadcasting Corporation) 39, 62–3, 67, 82
beat system 3, 12, 44
BetMGM 90
blogging *see* sports blogging
BlogHer 32
Boudway, I. 74
boundaries: athlete sports journalism 57–9, 61, 64; The Athletic 76–7, 80–1; background 3–4, 6–9, 10, 11; conclusions 97–9; COVID-19 and sports journalism 87–8; digital sports journalism 21, 24; sports blogging 28, 30, 35–8, 38–40; sports public relations 44–7, 49, 53, 55 *see also* access
Bourdieu, P. 6
Bournemouth Echo, The (known as *The Echo*) 54, 86
Boyle, R.: athlete sports journalism 57, 61, 67; future considerations 97, 100; sports journalists and the professional crisis 5, 12; sports public relations 46–7, 48
Bradshaw, T. 5, 76, 84, 90
brand image: building 75–6; and ethics 55–6; and legacy media 65; and loyalty 4; and market share 49; personal 34–5, 60, 61; public relations 43–4; and quality journalism 10, 81; strategies 99
Britain *see* UK

Index 119

British Broadcasting Corporation (BBC) 39, 62–3, 67, 82
broadcast versus print sports journalism 58–61
Burke, T. 30
Buzzelli, N.R. et al. 2, 72, 74, 75–6, 78, 80–1

Canada 33
Carlson, M. 6, 8, 21, 37
Carragher, Jamie 64–5, 67
Cavani, Edinson 19
changing boundaries of access 44–7
cheerleaders 3, 48, 51, 53, 56, 59, 85
Clavio, G. 73–4
clickbait 11, 22, 73, 75, 78, 80–1, 94
CNN (Cable News Network) 80, 85
codes of conduct 6
coercion 44, 54
complementary blogging 33–4
Conn, D. 83
content providers 20, 24
context: athlete sports journalism 57, 60; background 4–5, 7; conclusions 97, 99; COVID-19 and sports journalism 90; digital sports journalism 14, 21, 24; sports blogging 32; sports public relations 44
Cosell, H. 1
COVID-19 and sports journalism 82–93; athlete sports journalism 61; The Athletic 89–91; exclusive access: sports journalists in empty stadiums 87–9; future considerations 91–3, 95–6, 100; journalism and the return of sport 85–7; sports journalists and the professional crisis 11, 82–5
curation 4, 19, 24, 47, 94
Curtis, B. 59

Daily Mail 64, 71
Daily Mirror 84–5
Dart, J. 34
data visualisation 21
Daum, E.: digital sports journalism 14–16, 20, 22, 24; sports blogging 27, 33; sports public relations 44, 47, 49

Deadspin (US website) 28–32, 37, 40, 70, 98
Deuze, M. 8
Dickey, J. 30
digital and social media 2–3, 9, 13, 42, 48, 52
digital disruption to traditional practice 13–18
digital platforms: athlete sports journalism 67; The Athletic 69, 73–4; conclusions 95; digital sports journalism 13–14, 16, 20, 24–5; disruption to traditional practice 4; sports blogging 28–9, 40; sports public relations 49, 55–6
digital sports journalism 12–26; The Athletic 75; conclusions 23–6, 94, 100; digital disruption to traditional practice 13–18; emergence of the digital sports journalist 18–20; innovation or churnalism? 20–3; sports journalists and the professional crisis 12–13 see also digitally native sports journalists
digital technologies: athlete sports journalism 58; COVID-19 and sports journalism 88; digital sports journalism 12, 13–14, 21, 25; sports blogging 32; sports journalists and the professional crisis 2, 4–5, 7, 9–11; sports public relations 43–4, 52
digitally native sports journalists 3–4, 9, 12–13, 18–19, 24, 94 see also traditional sports journalists
disrupting sports journalism: athlete sports journalism 57–68; The Athletic 69–81; conclusions and future considerations 94–100; COVID-19 and sports journalism 82–93; digital sports journalism 12–26; sports blogging 27–41; sports journalists and the professional crisis 1–11; sports public relations 42–56
double sourcing (to corroborate information) 15
Dowling, D. 34–5, 75
Doyel, G. 85
Drellich, E. 77
due diligence 30

120 Index

Echo, The (Bournemouth Echo) 54, 86
EFL (English Football League) 82
Eldridge, S.A. 29, 37
embargos 37, 48, 59
emergence of the digital sports journalist 18–20
empty stadiums, sports journalists in 87–9
English Football League (EFL) 82
English, P. 8, 16
entertainment 14, 47, 58, 90, 94
EPL (Premier League) see Premier League (EPL)
Eriksson, G. 21
ESPN (Entertainment and Sports Programming Network) 19, 28, 30–1, 34–5, 60, 70–2
ethics: background 6, 8; COVID-19 and sports journalism 86, 91–2; digital sports journalism 15, 19; sports blogging 28–9, 38; sports public relations 45–6, 49, 51, 55–6
European Super League 100
Evetts, J. 8
evolution of sports journalism 97–9
exclusive access: sports journalists in empty stadiums 87–9

FA (Football Association) 19, 62, 83 see also Scottish Football Association (SFA)
Facebook Lives 18, 23
fact-checking 15, 22, 30
fake news 19
Fancy Bear 38, 98
female sports journalists 22, 45, 89
FIFA (Fédération Internationale de Football Association) 32, 50
Football Association (FA) 19, 62, 83 see also Scottish Football Association (SFA)
Football Leaks 38, 98
Football Ramble 39
Forde, S. 32, 98
Fox Sports 70–1
Franklin-Wallis, O. 70–1, 74, 76–7
future of access 96–7

Galily, Y. 25–6
Garrison, B. 1, 59

gatekeepers 3, 17, 37, 44, 48–9, 65, 96
gender discrimination 21–2, 45, 51, 61, 63
Gerrard, Steven 64–5
Ghana 34
Gieryn, T. 6–8
Godfrey, H. 89
Gold, A. 88
Grantland project 28, 34–5, 39
Great Britain see UK
Guardian Sports Network 28, 34, 38
Guardian, The 33–4, 38–9, 71–2, 83, 87

Hansmann, Adam 69, 90
Hardin, M. 32
Harris, Rob 53
Harrison, G. 46
HBO Sports 60, 63
hierarchies 17, 31, 96, 98
Higgerson, D. 53
hockey 65, 71, 76, 78, 87
Houghton, A. 77
Hutchins, B. 4, 19, 22, 48, 88

independence: athlete sports journalism 65; background 3, 5, 10; conclusions 95, 97; COVID-19 and sports journalism 91–2; sports blogging 29–30; sports public relations 42, 49, 51, 52–4, 55
India 23
Ingle, Sean 33
insider access 3–4, 17–18, 46, 77, 88, 98
Instagram 19, 51
interactive graphics 21
interloper media 25, 29–31, 80, 97, 100

James, L. 19, 74, 78
Joseph, S. 56

Kay-Jelski, A. 76, 90–1
Keown, Martin 64
Kroon, A. 21
Kunert, J. 25–6

Larson, M.S. 6
lay-offs 13, 25, 70, 76, 87, 91

Index 121

legacy media: athlete sports journalism 65; The Athletic 69–70, 72–6, 78–9, 80–1; digital sports journalism 20–1; future considerations 94–5, 98–9; sports blogging 31; sports public relations 49
legitimacy: athlete sports journalism 67; The Athletic 69; background 9–10; conclusions 99; COVID-19 and sports journalism 85; digital sports journalism 17, 18; sports blogging 35, 38–9; sports public relations 49–50
Leitch, Will 29, 35
Liew, Jonathan 39, 71–2
live blogging 21–2, 39, 94
long-form journalism: The Athletic 10, 69, 75, 78, 80–1; COVID-19 and sports journalism 90; digital sports journalism 20–1; sports blogging 35, 39; sports public relations 47
Lowes, M.: digital sports journalism 1, 12, 17; future considerations 94, 96–7; sports blogging 27, 37; sports public relations 47

MacIntyre, Darragh 63
Major League Soccer (MLS) 25, 87
major league sport 5, 15, 25, 44–5, 70, 77–8, 87
Manchester City 46–7, 51, 53, 78, 100
Manchester United 15–16, 19
Manti Te'o story 30–1
marginalised groups 21, 28, 34, 40, 43, 95, 96
Mason, Kate 39
Mather, Alex 69–70, 91
Mayhew, F. 84–5, 90
McEnnis, S. 36, 46
McGran, K. 87
media managers: The Athletic 78; background 3, 11; COVID-19 and sports journalism 85–6, 89; future considerations 97; sports blogging 40; sports public relations 43, 44–6, 48–9, 51–2, 54–5
media platforms 2–3, 43, 48–9

metrics-driven approaches 24, 74–5, 81, 94–5, 99
Microsoft Teams 88
Miller, T. 25, 100
Minogue, D. 5
Mirer, M. 48–50, 55
MLS (Major League Soccer) 25, 87
monopoly control 12, 23, 27, 37
Moritz, B. 12–13, 23, 73–4, 89, 92, 97
Morrison, S. 20–1
Mourinho, José 16, 47, 88
Muirhead, Andy 37
multimedia 13, 20–2, 35, 48–9, 75, 99

National Basketball Association (NBA) 46, 50–1, 71, 86
National Hockey League (NHL) 65, 87
NBA (National Basketball Association) 46, 50–1, 71, 86
Netflix 46, 60, 70
New York Times, The 20, 55, 63, 70
newspapers: athlete sports journalism 57–8, 59, 61, 64, 67; The Athletic 72, 75, 79; COVID-19 and sports journalism 86, 90; and digital platforms 3; digital sports journalism 16, 20, 21
NHL (National Hockey League) 65, 87
Nicholson, M. 17

objectivity: athlete sports journalism 61, 63–4, 67; digital sports journalism 17; future of access 97; sports blogging 30, 39; sports journalists and the professional crisis 2, 5, 8, 10; sports public relations 49, 53 *see also* subjectivity
occupational professionalism 13
Offside Rule Podcast 21
online sports journalism 2, 20
organisational professionalism 13
outsourcing 33, 98

pay cuts 91
paywalls 70, 72, 79–81
Petchesky, Barry 31
Philadelphia Inquirer, The 83, 86

Index

Pinto, Rui 38
Plimpton, George 65–6
Politi, S. 89
Premier League (EPL): athlete sports journalism 59, 62; The Athletic 71, 78; COVID-19 and sports journalism 82, 85, 88; digital sports journalism 15; sports public relations 47, 56
Press Association 23, 84
Press Gazette 84, 90
print versus broadcast sports journalism 58–61
professional practices 22, 76–9
professional standards 8, 12, 14, 23, 30, 39
promotional cultures 3, 43, 44, 46–7, 49, 52–4, 82
public service: athlete sports journalism 63; digital sports journalism 24; professional principles 5, 8, 98–9; sports public relations 10, 49, 52, 55
publicity agents 6, 55, 99
Pulitzer Prizes 20, 63
pundits 4, 51, 53, 61–2, 64–5, 66

racial abuse 19, 22, 63
radio 43, 54, 57, 60, 84, 86
Ramon, X. 15, 22, 29, 94
Reach plc 84–5
Redford, P. 76
redundancies 13, 25, 70, 76, 87, 91
Reed, S. 46
resistance from sports journalism to team media 51–4
restricted access 3, 15, 55, 89
return of sport, post-COVID-19 85–7, 91
Reuters 23
Rice, Grantland 28, 35
RioWatch 32
rise of athlete sports journalism 61–6
rise of team media 47–51
Robillard, C.: digital sports journalism 1, 12, 17; future considerations 94, 96–7; sports blogging 27, 37; sports public relations 47
Rojas-Torrijos, J. 21
role orientations 12, 24

Rosenthal, K. 71, 77
Rowe, D. 4, 19, 22, 32, 88

Salwen, M. 1, 59
Scherer, J.: digital sports journalism 14–16, 20, 22, 24; sports blogging 27, 33; sports public relations 44, 47, 49
Schwartz, D. 65
Scottish Football Association (SFA) 37 *see also* Football Association (FA)
Scotzine 37
Serazio, M. 29–31, 97
sexism 21–2, 45, 51, 61, 63
SFA (Scottish Football Association) 37 *see also* Football Association (FA)
Sherwood, M. 17, 43, 48, 52
Shorthand (multimedia storytelling software) 21
sign stealing 77
Simmons, Bill 34–5, 39
single sourcing (no corroboration of information) 15
SJA (Sports Journalists' Association) 50, 62, 79, 80
Sky Sports 15, 22, 39, 60–1, 63–4, 71, 82
Smith, A.B. 62, 65
social constructionism 9
social media: abuse 22; athlete sports journalism 59, 64, 67; The Athletic 70, 75, 81; COVID-19 and sports journalism 87; digital sports journalism 13, 14, 16–17, 19, 22, 23–4; future considerations 100; future of access 96; platforms 2, 3, 48; sports blogging 32, 37, 39; sports journalists and the professional crisis 5, 8, 9; sports public relations 42–3, 47–8, 51, 52–3, 55
sports blogging 27–41; as alternative sports journalism 28–33; background 27–8; blurring boundaries: sports journalist as blogger 38–40; conclusions 40–1; digital sports journalism 21–2; future considerations 94, 98; protecting boundaries from bloggers 35–8; sports

Index 123

journalism and acceptable blogging 33–5
Sports Illustrated 30, 66, 70–1, 79
Sports Journalism: Context and Issues (Boyle) 5
Sports Journalism: The State of Play (Bradshaw and Minogue) 5
sports journalists and the professional crisis 1–11; aims of the book 4–5; background 1–4; book outline 9–11; theoretical orientation 6–9
Sports Journalists' Association (SJA) 50, 62, 79, 80
sports public relations 42–56; background 42–4; changing access boundaries 44–7; conclusions 54–6; digital sports journalism 15; future considerations 94, 99–100; resistance from sports journalism 51–4; rise of team media 47–51; sports journalists and the professional crisis 3, 10
Strauss, B. 73–4, 79
subjectivity 2, 10, 14, 23, 31, 39–40, 67 *see also* objectivity
subscription-based models: The Athletic 10, 69–70, 72–4, 79–80; COVID-19 and sports journalism 90–1; future considerations 95, 97, 98
Sugden, J. 15, 60
Suggs Jr, D.W. 36, 44
Sun, The 36
Sunday Times, The 59, 66

Tameez, H. 83–4
team media: athlete sports journalism 65; COVID-19 and sports journalism 87, 93; digital technologies 3, 5, 10; future considerations 94, 96, 98–100; rise of 47–51; sports public relations 52, 55–6
technological determinism 9
Telegraph, The 64, 71–2, 79–80
television: athlete sports journalism 57–9, 60, 61–5, 67; The Athletic 77–8; changing journalistic practices 3–4, 7, 9; COVID-19 and sports journalism 82, 92; digital sports journalism 13, 16, 18, 21;

future considerations 96; sports blogging 27, 40; sports public relations 43, 45, 53
Te'o, Manti 30–1
The Players' Tribune 65
Therapeutic Use Exemptions (TUEs) 38, 66
Times, The 18, 38, 64, 71, 87
Tomlinson, A. 15, 60
Toronto Star, The 87
toy department reputation: The Athletic 73; COVID-19 and sports journalism 92; digital sports journalism 20; future considerations 94, 100; sports blogging 27, 30, 34, 38; sports journalists and the professional crisis 1–2, 4, 8
traditional sports journalists: athlete sports journalism 58, 63, 67–8; digital disruption to traditional practice 13–18; and digital sports journalism 12–13, 18–19, 21–2, 23–5; future considerations 95, 96–7; sports blogging 35–6; sports journalists and the professional crisis 3–4, 6–7, 9; sports public relations 48–9 *see also* digitally native sports journalists
TUEs (Therapeutic Use Exemptions) 38, 66
Tulloch, C.D. 15, 22, 29, 94
TV *see* television
Twitter: athlete sports journalism 59; The Athletic 70, 75, 76; digital sports journalism 12, 16–19, 23; sports blogging 35; sports public relations 51, 53

UK: athlete sports journalism 59–60, 61–4; The Athletic 69, 71–2, 76–7, 78, 80; COVID-19 and sports journalism 83–4, 86, 89–91; digital sports journalism 13, 15–16, 18, 21–3; sports blogging 28, 39; sports journalists and the professional crisis 5, 10; sports public relations 44, 46, 47, 50
US: athlete sports journalism 59–60, 62–3, 65–6; The Athletic 69–72, 78–9; COVID-19 and sports

journalism 89–91; digital sports journalism 12, 15, 20; sports blogging 28–9, 32, 34, 36; sports journalists and the professional crisis 1, 5, 10; sports public relations 44, 49

verification 22–3
Vimieiro, A.C. 31
Vogan, T. 34–5, 65, 75

Wall, M. 7
Walsh, David 66
Warner, J. 66
Washington Post, The 25, 71
Whiteside, E. 62, 65
Wilson, B. 32, 98
Winter, Henry 18, 71
women sports journalists 22, 45, 89
work routines 9, 23, 42, 93, 97
Wright, Ian 62

YouTube videos 4, 19, 23

Zelizer, B. 7
Zoom 11, 88–9